Voices of Influence

NATIONAL ASSOCIATION OF TEACHERS OF SINGING BOOKS
The National Association of Teachers of Singing (NATS) publishes high-quality books for singers, teachers, and other voice professionals. NATS books provide valuable and trusted resources that enhance singing pedagogy and support the important work of all singing professionals.

NATS is the leading professional organization devoted to the science and art of singing.

ABOUT THE NATIONAL ASSOCIATION OF TEACHERS OF SINGING
Founded in 1944, the National Association of Teachers of Singing (NATS) is the world's largest professional association of voice teachers and collaborative pianists with more than seven thousand members in the United States, Canada, and more than thirty-five other countries. Whether working in independent studios, community schools, elementary and secondary schools, higher education, or in the medical field, NATS members represent the diversity of today's music landscape, teaching in all musical styles. For more information, visit NATS.org.

RECENTLY PUBLISHED NATS BOOKS
Practical Vocal Acoustics: Pedagogic Applications for Teachers and Singers by
    Kenneth Bozeman
The Functional Unity of the Singing Voice, Second Edition Expanded
    by Barbara Doscher
Trauma and the Voice: A Guide for Singers, Teachers, and Other Practitioners,
    edited by Emily Jaworski Koriath
The Singing Book, Fourth Edition by Cynthia Vaugh and Meribeth Dayme,
    edited by Matthew Hoch
*Unlocking Meaning in Art Song: A Singer's Guide to Practical Analysis Using Schubert
    Songs* by Beverly Stein

Voices of Influence

Exploring the Journey of a Teacher and Student in the Voice Studio

Brian Manternach

BLOOMSBURY ACADEMIC
NEW YORK · LONDON · OXFORD · NEW DELHI · SYDNEY

BLOOMSBURY ACADEMIC

Bloomsbury Publishing Inc, 1359 Broadway, New York, NY 10018, USA
Bloomsbury Publishing Plc, 50 Bedford Square, London, WC1B 3DP, UK
Bloomsbury Publishing Ireland, 29 Earlsfort Terrace, Dublin 2, D02 AY28, Ireland

BLOOMSBURY, BLOOMSBURY ACADEMIC and the Diana logo are trademarks of Bloomsbury Publishing Plc

First published in the United States of America 2025

Copyright © The National Association of Teachers of Singing, 2025

For legal purposes the Acknowledgments on p. xi constitute an extension of this copyright page.

Cover design: Sally Rinehart
Cover image © iStock.com/gmalandra

All rights reserved. No part of this publication may be: i) reproduced or transmitted in any form, electronic or mechanical, including photocopying, recording or by means of any information storage or retrieval system without prior permission in writing from the publishers; or ii) used or reproduced in any way for the training, development or operation of artificial intelligence (AI) technologies, including generative AI technologies. The rights holders expressly reserve this publication from the text and data mining exception as per Article 4(3) of the Digital Single Market Directive (EU) 2019/790.

Bloomsbury Publishing Inc does not have any control over, or responsibility for, any third-party websites referred to or in this book. All internet addresses given in this book were correct at the time of going to press. The author and publisher regret any inconvenience caused if addresses have changed or sites have ceased to exist, but can accept no responsibility for any such changes.

Library of Congress Cataloging-in-Publication Data

ISBN: HB: 979-8-7651-4612-5
PB: 979-8-7651-4611-8
ePub: 979-8-7651-4614-9
ePDF: 979-8-7651-4613-2

Typeset by Deanta Global Publishing Services, Chennai, India
Printed and bound in the United States of America

For product safety related questions contact productsafety@bloomsbury.com.

To find out more about our authors and books visit www.bloomsbury.com and sign up for our newsletters.

Contents

Preface: Professional Biography of Dr. Robert J. Harrison vii
Foreword ix
Acknowledgments xi

Introduction: Like Teacher, Like Student: Pedagogy through Story and Personal History 1

Part I The Journey

1. When the Student Is Ready, the Teacher Will Appear: Finding the Right Fit 11

2. Early Influences and Examples: The Importance of Curiosity, Mentors, and Role Models 17

3. Professional Life: First Jobs, Dealing with Rejection, and Personal Sacrifice for Professional Gain 33

Part II Lessons, Philosophies, and Practices

4. Embracing Eccentricities: "Sometimes, to make a point, you have to make a circus." 49

5. Learning via the Senses: Developing a Detail-Oriented Mind 53

6. "What Is an Art Song, Anyway?": Intellectual Enlightenment and Musical Bias 61

7. Selfless Communication: Teaching Artistry 73

8 Respiration: No Air, No Sound 83

9 Balanced Phonation: SOVTEs, Negotiating the *Passaggio*, and Exercising the Whole Voice 97

10 A Vowel-Based Approach to Resonance: Assessing Pressure versus Flow 103

11 Choosing Purposeful Exercises: Listening as the First Step to Problem-Solving 111

12 Learning, Questioning, and Dealing with Doubt: "Verify It" 119

13 Prioritizing Teaching: Professing Truth 125

14 What Makes a Good Student? What Makes a Good Teacher? 131

Part III Legacy

15 On the Shoulders of Giants: Assessing, Evaluating, and Citing 139

16 How to Fairly Evaluate: Contextualizing a Career 145

17 Judicious Emulation: When to Turn Away from What We Were Taught 149

18 Conclusion: My Teacher's Student 153

Appendix I: *Nacht und Träume* 161
Appendix II: A Brief Timeline of the Life and Career of Dr. Robert J. Harrison 172
Appendix III: Final Quotes 174
Bibliography 176
Contributors 180
Index 183

Preface
Professional Biography of Dr. Robert J. Harrison

D.M.A., University of Arizona, 1986
M.M., UW-Madison, 1978
B.A., Milton College, 1971

- Freelance chorister, New York City, under Leonard Bernstein, Robert Shaw, Leopold Stokowski, Dave Brubeck, Gregg Smith, and Eve Queler
- Performer at the White House for President Richard Nixon
- Professor, Indiana University Jacobs School of Music, Bloomington (2004–15)
- Professor, University of Colorado Boulder (1981–2004)
- Performances at national conferences for the National Association of Teachers of Singing (NATS), College Music Society (CMS), and Midwest Historical Keyboard Society (MHKS)
- Master Teacher, NATS Intern Program (2002)
- Master classes and presentations at the American Academy (Rome), Universidad Nacional de San Juan (Argentina), American University (Cairo), Real Conservatorio Superior de Musica (Madrid), Conservatori de Musica del Liceu (Barcelona), Hochschule für Musik Hanns Eisler (Berlin), Festival Internacional de Inverno de Campos do Jordão (Brazil)
- Student awards/performances: Truman Scholar Award, Metropolitan Opera National Council, Denver Lyric Opera Guild, San Francisco Opera, Palm Beach Opera, Music Academy of the West, Komische Oper Berlin, Lyric Opera of Chicago, Atlanta Opera, Utah Opera, Central City Opera, Opera Colorado, Staatsoper Hamburg, Opera New Jersey, New York City Opera, Santa Fe Opera, Glimmerglass Opera, Seattle Opera, Ohio Light Opera, Boston Symphony, New York Philharmonic, Tanglewood, Philadelphia Orchestra, Cincinnati Orchestra, Caramoor

Festival, Aldeburgh Festival, Mostly Mozart Festival of Lincoln Center, PBS Great Performances, and appearances on Broadway
  - Full-time choristers within the chorus of the Metropolitan Opera
  - Two IMG artists
  - Students teaching at colleges and universities across the United States
- One of the fourteen voice teachers featured in the book *Great Teachers on Great Singing* by Robin Rice (2017)
- He and his wife, Sandra, are retired and reside in Castle Pines, Colorado, near their much-loved grandchildren, Violet and Liam.
- Teaching philosophy posted on his studio door:

  If you love your art, you will work despite obstacles and love it. If you have to be prodded to it, better choose an easier gesture to express yourself. Art offers no crown for mediocrity. (Geraldine Farrar, soprano)

Figure P.1 Robert J. Harrison in the early 1990s, with his left hand on a 1702 score of Henry Purcell's *Orpheus Britannicus*.

Foreword

In 2004, I applied for a job posted as either an assistant or associate professor of voice at Indiana University, my graduate school alma mater. Based on the job description, I knew they were looking for an established teacher—someone who could teach applied lessons, vocal pedagogy, and/or other voice-related courses. Of course, IU has a history of hiring professors who have built significant reputations as performers on the international opera stage, which is a selling point for many of the students who attend. I had never earned my income principally through performance, so on paper, I wasn't particularly confident that I would be considered. I did have a record of solid teaching, however, and since the need in the school that year seemed to be for more of an academic, I felt I could make the best case for myself if I was able to demonstrate that in person.

As the process went forward, I was invited for an on-campus interview, which included presenting a pedagogy lecture, teaching a master class, and performing a mini-recital. At the time, I remember thinking to myself, "They're not looking at you to be the name on the marquee. Just go there and *teach*." I was offered the job and happily joined the faculty of the Department of Voice, for which I now serve as chair.

The same year, Robert Harrison was hired for a second, more senior position (full professor) on the voice faculty. I knew Bob by reputation since he had previously served as a master teacher for the NATS Intern Program. When I met him at a faculty gathering the day before classes started in fall 2004, he seemed like somebody I could relate to, since we had both come from academia rather than the performance world.

When I am out recruiting for the Jacobs School of Music, I emphasize the importance of the teacher-student dynamic. Instinct is incredibly important in making these decisions, but instinct can sometimes be too heavily guided by emotion. I encourage prospective students to decide what their priorities are, consider what they're looking for, and then seek a teacher who shares those priorities. One of the benefits we have at Indiana is a large and diverse faculty. Every teacher has had success, despite working from sometimes differing philosophies. I frequently say to prospective students, "I'm butter pecan, but if you want strawberry or chocolate chip, that's right down the hall. Go get it!"

This book analyzes the teacher-student dynamic, as told through the relationship the author, Brian Manternach, developed during his time as Bob's student at IU and continuing on beyond that. Although it focuses on experiences based on this particular relationship, the writing explores inner, universal themes and touches on them in a way that individuals will find immediately relatable to their own lives—as I did. The book will specifically resonate with those who teach in one-on-one situations, whether that be in an applied music studio (vocal or instrumental), in athletic coaching or training, or in similar teacher-student settings.

Despite IU Opera Theater's well-established reputation for excellence, Brian did not come here to launch a career as an opera singer; he came here to be part of the overall atmosphere and to learn and absorb as much as possible. He did so with character, bravery, and the inner confidence that he could be successful. Although it was not without its sacrifices, he found a way to forge a career that is entirely his own, which I have always admired about him. In so doing, he was savvy enough to identify Bob as a great teacher but, more importantly, the *right* teacher for him.

As chair of this department, it makes me understandably proud to see our graduates—like Larry Brownlee and Jamie Barton, to name only two—having such success on the operatic stage. I am equally proud to see graduates like Dr. Manternach who are teaching the next generation of singers and scholars in extraordinary, though perhaps not as celebrated, ways. His writing—in *Classical Singer*, the NATS *Journal of Singing*, and in this book—is relatable, erudite, and compelling.

Brian Horne, D. M.
Chair, Department of Voice,
Indiana University Jacobs School of Music

Acknowledgments

Brian

Since this is a book about teachers, I would be remiss not to mention the knowledgeable, dedicated, patient music teachers I have benefited from throughout my formal music education: Mrs. Paulson, Mrs. Conley, Mrs. Knuth, Mr. Stanaway, Mr. Warner, Mr. Ewan, Mr. Marshall, Prof. Dewese, Dr. Finley, Dr. Theimer, Prof. Welter, Dr. Koopman, Dr. Lavonis, Dr. Errante, Dr. Hansen, Dr. Burkholder, Prof. Kiesgen, Prof. Hart, Dr. Horne, and, *natürlich*, Dr. Harrison.

I am also indebted to my research mentors and valued collaborators, Dr. Ingo Titze, Dr. Lynn Maxfield, and Dr. Jeremy Manternach. Thanks especially to Lynn and Jeremy for reviewing some of the more technical sections of this book. Thanks as well to Michael Tan and the entire team at Bloomsbury Academic for their expert guidance throughout the publication process.

Thank you to the University of Utah Department of Theatre, the Utah Center for Vocology, and the Summer Vocology Institute for giving me a place to do what I love, and thank you to my students for allowing me to engage with people I love.

My greatest debt (personal and professional) is to Erika, my life partner and, conveniently, my in-house copyeditor. Not a word that I write goes out to the public before passing before her eyes. She continues to bring clarity to my writing, my thoughts, and my life.

Erika

As described in this story, I was not present for most of the moments that cemented the friendship and mentor/mentee connection between Brian and Bob due to the distance between our home in the South Bend area and Bob's studio in Bloomington, Indiana. However, I have certainly witnessed the impact their relationship had on Brian's teaching philosophies, personal artistry, and values. Meeting and working with Bob was a game-changer for Brian and, therefore, for us.

In addition to all the ways you will read that they are alike, I offer two more. First, they both have an unwavering sense of who they are, and while they are not unaffected by criticism or self-doubt, they are more comfortable in their own skin than most people I know. Brian says Bob is "insistently himself," and I think the description fits Brian, too. He is who he is. He was before he met Bob, but I have to believe they recognize and magnify that admirable trait in each other. Though not intransigent, they are both pretty unflappable in the face of judgment, which gives them the freedom to take big risks.

They both also have the courage to confront their own failures and shortcomings personally and publicly. They have the guts to say, "I tried to do this and failed. I learned from it and I'm not ashamed of it." This is a gift for their students and colleagues, to say nothing of their life partners.

These are just two reasons why I love them both. I am proud to have contributed in a small way to this examination of their relationship, and I thank my own family, teachers, mentors, and employers who have helped me develop the skills to make such a collaboration possible.

Bob

Although my gratitude might be of insufficient length to the reader, know it contains a depth of indebtedness that is unspeakably profound. All listed below have shaped my life, my thinking, and my entire being in many beautiful, humbling, and enlightening ways. To:

Brian and Erika, who so wonderfully organized and composed this book about the journey of an extraordinarily complicated individual and his accomplished study—and to do so in such a manner to humble and emotionally disrupt me;

Dame Elizabeth Schwarzkopf, there was not a day of my work when I did not look upon you as the sole example of how to communicate the language of music;

Vance Yoder George, who recognized my talent when I was a high school student and who invited me to be a member of the UW-Madison Tudor Singers at the age of sixteen;

All of my past students, who shared their deep respect for and truthful performances of music and who trusted me;

The IU students of all areas of musical study; from my first day on campus, you demonstrated your respect for my teaching, further addressing me as *maestro*, a title of the highest honor; the title came with a responsibility to become a better one;

CU Professors Alan A. Luhring and Howard B. Waltz, who taught me that the thoughts of composers are revealed in their musical scores and who guided me through the harsh maze of academia; thank you, Alan, for advising me often that "CU's a very good place to be from." Howard, you guided me as a most loving father;

Professor of English Audrey Eiler, who so caringly and challengingly taught me to respect and write well the English language; the D- you rightly inked upon my report card was an appropriate, accurate, and motivating measurement;

CU Professor of Guitar, Charles Wolzien, my voice-guitar partner and multi-stylist and historian for over a decade, you can really play *the ax*, Chucky; because solely of you, we enjoyed some wonderful tours together;

IU Professors Costanza Cuccaro and Paul Kiesgen, for your unflagging trust in and respect for my work—enough so, you led the IU search committee to recommend my appointment to the IU faculty;

Emeritus IU Dean Gwyn Richards, for your measured support of my appointment;

CU Professors Thomas Binkley (Early Music Institute) and Hans Tischler (Musicology): without your letters of full support for my work, I would have never achieved tenure and promotion at CU Boulder.

*

Mother and Dad, you gave me the wings and blue skies with and in which to fly and did so with much love, tolerance, and compassion;

Joanna, Lilly, Mark, Violet, and Liam, you give me heaps of pride and much unconditional love—and above all, much hope. All of you own a significant piece of this book;

Most of all to my wife, Sandy, who, when I proposed to you on July 23, 1971, in Fox Point, Wisconsin, your eyes and heart expressed ever brightly that you loved me and that you would love me, so unconditionally, forever.

In memory of
Gracie and Ruby

Figure 0.1 Erika, Bob, and Brian in Denver, Colorado, May 2017.

Introduction
Like Teacher, Like Student: Pedagogy through Story and Personal History

October 2, 2020

Dear lovely friends,

I write this letter to both of you, and it is not an easy one to lay out, so I shall cut to the chase! As you know, I had a near-40-year career in academia. Over those years, my students needled me to write a book. To this day, now and then, a former student will ask that I write one. In no way, shape, or form is my thinking organized to launch into a book project. And at my age, 71, I haven't a modicum of interest in producing one. I would rather count the peaks of the Rocky Mountain range!

With some chagrin, I come to you two. If a book were to be written about me and my work, I can think of no individuals who know me better, know the art of music better, and who could organize my disorganized life and work better than you two. Does this kind of a project have the interest required to bring a project like this to fruition? Is the time required for such a project worth your time and joint talents? Give it some thought—and take your time doing so—and in no way feel hesitant to give me your most honest NO.

Love to you both.

Bob

Erika and I were a bit surprised to receive this out-of-the-blue message from Bob. He was my teacher, mentor, and primary advisor during my doctoral studies at the Indiana University Jacobs School of Music in Bloomington. We had two years of voice lessons as part of my coursework from 2004 to 2006, and he continued to serve as my committee chair until I completed the degree in 2009. We have often been in touch since then, even after his retirement in 2015, and I continue to regard him as one of the most influential teachers I have had. He has written numerous letters of recommendation for me. We have had many conversations about the arts, music, and academia (and politics, and religion, and life in general), and he has never been shy to advocate on my behalf and celebrate my successes.

Of course, we were honored to know that Bob would entrust us with such a project. But we also knew that to do it justice would be a significant undertaking. Knowing how much we both admire the man, it would be a labor of love, to be certain. But still, labor, nonetheless. We talked through our initial questions. Is this a project worth doing? Absolutely. Could we set aside the time to do it? Probably, if we could take it at our own pace. How would we work out the division of labor? As Bob's student, I could serve as the author, and Erika, as a professional writer and copyeditor, could proof and polish what I had written.

There was one other question I had, which Bob also articulated in our subsequent conversations: Is there an audience for a book like this? As an avid reader and a book-review columnist for *Classical Singer* magazine, I have an understanding of the publication landscape in the area of singing and vocal pedagogy. There are several books on my shelf that were written to highlight celebrated singers and pedagogues and to share the techniques and methodologies they espouse. In fact, Bob is profiled in one of these books already, in a chapter of *Great Teachers on Great Teaching* by Robin Rice (Inside View Press, 2017).

As his former student, I am a firsthand witness to the efficacy of his teaching. I could easily and enthusiastically write an homage to my beloved mentor, sharing the best of his teaching that so powerfully influenced my life in music. But does the field really need another teacher-tribute book? And, to be frank, is he well-known enough to garner widespread interest? Bob spent the majority of his career teaching at highly regarded schools of music—first at the University of Colorado Boulder, in the pedagogical lineage of Berton Coffin (1910–87) and Barbara Doscher (1922–96), and then at the Indiana

University Jacobs School of Music, with its long history of renowned faculty and successful graduates in opera and classical singing. However, Bob did not have an international performing career, never published a book or major papers in peer-reviewed journals, and never worked the lecture circuit at festivals and conferences. I wholeheartedly believe his life and career are worth profiling, but would others think so?

As I spent some time reflecting on my studies with Bob, more than fifteen years removed from my last voice lesson, I found that I had fewer and fewer memories of the specific techniques we worked on. I remember feeling at the time that his teaching methods were solid and based on the best information available at the time (they were both evidence-based and science-informed before the field of voice pedagogy had adopted those terms). I also noted that there were specific parallels in our journeys through life and music that seemed to contribute to us being a good fit for each other.

But I also felt, even back then, that what made him an effective teacher went beyond mere technique. What has stuck with me over the years are his overarching philosophies, the life experiences he shared that formed those philosophies, and the larger-than-life personality traits that make Bob Bob. In short, by welcoming me into the approach he used to become an artist, I had an example, if not a blueprint, to become an artist myself. It wasn't a step-by-step guide or a mere checklist. Rather, it was built upon a lifetime of noticing followed by concentrated listening and then studying in order to inform future noticing and concentrated listening.

In our initial discussions with Bob, he was adamant that we should take the book in whatever direction we felt would be most interesting to us and to a potential audience. He was clear that he had no interest in simply a celebration of his professional success. Rather, since so many of his former students had told him how unique and impactful his teaching had been, he felt a book could be one more chance to share his perspectives with a wider audience, should there be a desire to hear them.

Therefore, I have decided to divide the book into three primary sections. In Part I (Chapters 1–3), I look at "who Bob is," exploring how he thinks, what he believes, and how that has informed his life as an artist and as a teacher. This includes some background on how he was raised and educated and identifying which of his early experiences were most formative to his musical life.

In Part II (Chapters 4–14), I dig into "what Bob taught." This includes some technical talk, examining Bob's thoughts on respiration, phonation, resonance, registration, and articulation, and how his understanding of these elements informed his choices in the studio. I also include a discussion of how he taught artistry, from how he defines his own musical tastes and sensibilities to how he taught communicative singing in seeking to help students "lift the music off the page." Along the way, I explore further some of his core philosophies and present some of his trademark phrases—the "Bob-isms" that many of his students will recognize.

In Part III (Chapters 15–18), I examine the complicated idea of "legacy." I consider how we might remember our teachers and their influence once their formal instruction has concluded. I also consider how to contextualize the work of teachers from previous generations in order to fairly assess their contributions.

Additionally, I will add my own background, reflections, and perspectives throughout this book. This allows me to present how Bob's instruction has merged with my own experiences and understandings, and how that filters into the information and practices I bring to my students. I do this a bit sheepishly, understanding that it may read as though I am inserting myself into his story—and, indeed, that may be exactly what I'm doing. But, in discussing Applied Lessons with Bob, it seems important to include how his lessons are actually applied. As an educator myself, I know that the only true measure of the effect of our teaching is how it impacts our students. Some of these impacts are immediately observable, some are only revealed if articulated to us by our students, and some (perhaps most) emerge over time in such a way that we may never even know about them. The old adage that a teacher's influence never stops is certainly true of Bob's influence on me, as I continue to ruminate on all he still teaches me. Therefore, this book is essentially a case study of one teacher-student dynamic and how information, philosophies, and practices change and (hopefully) evolve as they are passed along in the educational chain. As such, it is part memoir, part coming-of-age story, and part pedagogical guide—thus the title of this book: *Voices of Influence: Exploring the Journey of a Teacher and Student in the Voice Studio*.

Of course, I also have to acknowledge that some of the lessons we inadvertently teach our students are how not to do things. Indeed, learning from our teachers' missteps (failures, even) and exploring the areas where we disagree may be some of the most lasting lessons we can gain from their instruction. Some of what I do in the studio is my best attempt to imitate Bob, while some of what I do is in direct, conscious opposition to his teaching. In both cases, through me, his influence impacts an entirely new generation of singers (a realization and responsibility that I hold with overwhelming respect and humility).

Singers and teachers are storytellers. We know that everyone has a different, unique, and valuable history. It is my hope that by sharing stories and anecdotes related to my path, Bob's path, and our shared path, you may come to value your own path (however circuitous), realize a deeper appreciation for your influential mentors and unique experiences, and view even painful rejections as valuable, formative elements of your life—both personal and professional. I hope you will also feel encouraged to know that everyone's path is different and that there are few mandatory boxes to check in order to achieve your own version of success in this field.

In addition, as artists, we value process, not just product. A crucial element of the process of learning is how lessons are passed from teacher to student, which often occurs through story. The way the lessons of these stories embed themselves in a student's understanding—enhancing that student's skill set—is often inextricably linked to personal history and the relationship of teacher and student. It is the element of one-on-one studio instruction that exceeds the transactional and is difficult to accurately measure or quantify. I hope that readers will find pedagogical value not just in the philosophies, techniques, and tactics discussed in this book but also in the stories through which they are told. By highlighting the personal history and connection that made these lessons so impactful for me, as Bob's student, I hope you will consider the stories that influenced you and will feel emboldened to share them with your students as ways to both instruct and connect.

Caveat Emptor

I should mention a couple of caveats before beginning in earnest. First, I expect that Bob and I will both eventually shift the way we feel about some of what we advocate in this book. While he adamantly still believes in some of the perspectives and practices he shared, others—seen through a modern lens—cause him to wonder if they were the best choices. In that way, we should approach them much the way we approach performances: they serve as a snapshot in time, a reflection of the best we can do in a single moment, alongside all our imperfections, and knowing that our thoughts and capabilities will continue to evolve. Therefore, buyers beware. We could change our minds on these practices and philosophies as we gain new perspectives and experiences. Though we hope you will entertain and consider our thoughts, you are free to disagree with any of what we say.

Second, much of the information in this book is taken from almost twenty hours of interviews with Bob, completed over Zoom between October 2020 and March 2023. I recorded and transcribed every interview, and the quotes from Bob are taken directly from those transcriptions. These quotes were sometimes lightly edited to provide context or continuity. Much of the book also draws from memory, both Bob's and my own. Of course, memory is notoriously fallible. As neuroscientist Daniela Schiller points out, the process of recalling a memory can actually change it. "We don't really remember the original; we remember the revised version," she says.[1] I have made every effort to relate stories to the best of my recollection, without embellishment. But I also acknowledge that, as well-known stories and experiences become lore, they sometimes take on additional details. Apologies for any unintended inaccuracies.

Third, Bob and I agree that students should be cautioned against simply emulating their teachers. It is not our goal to mold students into carbon copies of ourselves. I hope that all teachers would want their students to build upon and adjust what they have learned in ways that serve their own performance goals and/or instructional goals. When particular tactics or techniques do not serve them, those tactics and techniques should absolutely be adjusted or discarded. It is nonsensical to continue to advocate an inadequate practice simply because it is how we were taught. At the outset of this project, Bob said to me—as he did to all of his students—"Question and check everything I say," so I do not hesitate to highlight areas where he and I diverge.

In our time together, Bob has been extremely complimentary of my skills and my impact in the field, and he has often provided validation and encouragement to me as an artist and a scholar in times when I needed to hear them. There is a well-known phrase, most often attributed to activist and author Maya Angelou: "At the end of the day, people won't remember what you said or did, they will remember how you made them feel." Certainly, there were individual days when I left voice lessons with Bob not feeling particularly good about my voice, my potential, or my path, even if those days were not the norm. If every lesson is a perfect lesson, it may mean we aren't being challenged enough as students. However, the days I left his studio feeling inspired and capable of working toward the improvement I desired were much more numerous. Ultimately, when I reflect on our time together, I am filled with gratitude that our paths converged.

Therefore, once again, buyers beware. This book is written with unchecked and unapologetic bias. I hold a tremendous amount of love for this quirky, eccentric, imperfect, outstanding teacher and bighearted man. I hope that when he reads through these pages, it will make his heart smile. And I hope the rest of you can feel just a bit of that love and take it into your own work as singers and teachers.

Note

1 Daniela Schiller as quoted in Susan Young Rojahn, "Memory Is Inherently Fallible, and That's a Good Thing," *MIT Technology Review*, October 9, 2013, https://www.technologyreview.com/2013/10/09/176152/memory-is-inherently-fallible-and-thats-a-good-thing/ (accessed November 14, 2024).

Part I
The Journey

1 When the Student Is Ready, the Teacher Will Appear

Finding the Right Fit

In the summer of 1996, I arrived on the campus of the University of Colorado Boulder to participate in the Colorado Lyric Theatre Festival. I had just finished my junior year of college as a vocal performance major at the College of Saint Benedict and Saint John's University—partner liberal arts colleges in central Minnesota. I was excited for my first out-of-state, paid gig ("paid," in this case, meaning provided housing and a modest stipend for the seven-week program).

I also knew that I would be applying for graduate programs after I finished my bachelor's degree, so I was considering the summer an extended college visit. The advice I constantly received was that, for graduate programs in voice performance, the most important element to consider is the studio teacher with whom I would study in private voice lessons. Once I settled in and rehearsals had started, I decided to reach out to a few members of the voice faculty to inquire about taking summer lessons. Given that I would be there for several weeks, I was hoping to take a series of voice lessons with a couple of teachers rather than just a handful of one-off trial lessons. In my thinking, that would be the best way to evaluate the progress I may be able to make with these teachers once we progressed beyond the introductory phase of instruction.

During my undergraduate studies, I took applied voice lessons from two wonderful teachers, baritone Scott Dewese and soprano Carolyn Finley. Both helped me immensely as this ambitious but naive youngster from rural Iowa began to discover what it meant to be a music major and what a life and career in music could be. Under their care and supervision, and in the supportive environment the schools offer, I slowly started to mature as a musician and student. By my junior year, I knew that I wanted to pursue graduate studies immediately after I finished college—partly because I was eager to learn more and continue progressing, and partly because I felt I had the energy and momentum to take that next step, in contrast to the school-induced burnout some of my classmates were feeling.

For my next degree, I was looking for a tenor who could serve as my voice teacher. I was hoping that someone who shares my voice type would have personal experiences and insights as to how I might negotiate my developing voice as well as possess in-depth knowledge of the tenor repertoire I was hoping to perform. There was one tenor on the voice faculty at CU. So, one day before rehearsal, I found the studio door bearing the name of Robert J. Harrison. When I knocked, the door was quickly opened, and I was greeted by a smiling man whose stature did nothing to refute the stereotype of tenors lacking height. He was bespectacled with frames that embodied the Oscar Wilde quote, "One should either be a work of art, or wear a work of art" (I would later learn that the man standing before me was a living example of both the former and the latter). Lest there be any doubt, the pitch and volume of his first spoken words made it clear that, if there was one tenor on the faculty, it had to be him.

I don't remember much of the content of our first conversation, which is unsurprising since first takeaways from interactions with Bob are often about the personality and flair with which his words are delivered rather than the message of what he is saying. I do remember him being friendly (jovial, even) and kind. When I explained that I was in town to work with the Colorado Lyric Theatre Festival and asked if he would be willing to take on a voice student for the summer, he told me that, regrettably, his studio was full, so he would not be able to take on another student. At that point, I should have asked about scheduling a single trial lesson, but I didn't have the foresight to make that request. Regardless, he recommended I approach his colleague, soprano Patti Peterson, to see if she might be able to take on a student for the summer. I followed his advice and had a series of productive lessons with Dr. Peterson, further preparing me for my senior year of college and my graduate school auditions.

During my subsequent trip to Boulder to formally audition for the program, the days were too busy to fit in trial lessons, so I never did get to sing for Bob. At the end of my audition process, I was fortunate enough to have received four acceptance letters, all of which were solid options for graduate schools I could have easily envisioned myself pursuing. Ultimately, upon considering all the pros and cons, I decided against CU, choosing instead to attend the University of Wisconsin-Milwaukee, where tenor William Lavonis expertly guided me through the next stage of my vocal and artistic development. But I always knew I would have had a positive experience in Colorado, had I decided to go that route.

Fast-forward to the summer of 2004. Having been accepted into the doctoral voice program at the Indiana University Jacobs School of Music, I had enthusiastically enrolled and was eager to absorb as much as I could from the program. Remembering the advice from years earlier, I had two teachers on my list of potential applied voice instructors, both tenors with whom I had taken trial lessons and knew would be wonderful guides in my vocal progress. The first teacher had been on sabbatical the previous year and I had a difficult time getting a hold of him—several emails and voice messages went unanswered. I finally learned the reason for this lack of communication when he eventually contacted me late in the spring to say that he was leaving IU for a position at another university. At this late stage, I reached out to the second teacher on my list, but his fall studio was already full.

So there I was, going back to school for a terminal degree in vocal performance with no idea who my voice instructor would be—flying in the face of the advice I was given over and over again that the studio teacher was the most important component of graduate work in voice. Luckily, the music office at IU informed me that there were two new hires in the voice department (both of them tenors!), Brian Horne and Robert Harrison. Hoping to schedule trial lessons with both teachers but remembering my time in Colorado, I decided to first see if this was the same Robert Harrison I had briefly met in Boulder. When I went to his studio and the door was opened, I was once again greeted by the same stout man in noteworthy glasses (a decidedly flashier pair than I remembered from Colorado). I reintroduced myself, described our last encounter, and explained that I was in need of a teacher as I was beginning my doctoral studies. We set up an appointment for a trial lesson, where he made it clear that we would both be looking to determine whether we were a good fit for each other. He in no way expected that I would simply join his studio, at this point in my studies, without an opportunity to work together first.

Once again, I don't remember a lot of specifics about what we worked on in that first lesson. I couldn't tell you what particular areas of technique or artistry we addressed or even what music I sang. But I remember feeling that he was someone from whom I could learn a tremendous amount, who would challenge me to think deeply, and who would help me develop as an artist and not just as a singer. When he offered me a place in his studio, I accepted it on the spot. Though I never did schedule a voice lesson with Brian Horne, I am grateful that he also became an important mentor to me, both during my time at IU and in the years since I graduated.

By joining Bob's studio in his first semester in Bloomington, I became his first IU doctoral student, a distinction I carry with a degree of pride. I recall many times during my coursework, in conversations with classmates, when the inevitable question would come up: "Who is your voice teacher?" When I would answer, "Dr. Harrison," I was, in the beginning, usually met with blank stares or responses of "Who is that?" Bob's hire did not cause a big splash, by IU standards, since he wasn't pulled from the upper echelon of operatic performance (a hiring trend IU has long followed). Instead, he had come from the world of academia, as did Brian Horne. Arguably, two hires in the same year from academia rather than the performance world actually was the sort of move that should be considered a big splash, especially for IU. For a school that has a reputation for hiring world-renowned performers, hiring two faculty members who had spent their careers dedicated to teaching rather than exclusively to performing was a significant statement.

Regardless, due to Bob's lack of name recognition, one classmate told me at the time, "He's lucky to have you. As a new teacher, he probably has mostly undergraduates." Although I'm sure the comment was intended as a compliment to me, it didn't sit well. First, why should teaching undergraduate students be seen as less gratifying or less important than working with graduate students? Second, as I was told from the beginning, students should do their homework when looking for a studio teacher, in part because of the importance of finding someone who is the right "fit." If someone like Bob, with more than twenty-five years (at that point) of teaching success—working with undergraduate through doctoral students—is written off as a potential teacher because he has never performed at the Metropolitan Opera, that would seem to speak to the ignorance of the students choosing studio teachers rather than any perceived ineptitude of the teacher.

Later in this book, I will discuss whether great performers can become great teachers. So as not to keep anyone in suspense, they absolutely can and frequently do. But, as those accomplished performers-turned-teachers will likely confess, teaching and performing are incredibly different skills. (Note the intentional use of the word "skills," meaning something to be developed over time, as opposed to "talents," implying something inherent.) Although we all have different natural capabilities, both performing and teaching are skills. Success in one area does not guarantee equal success in the other. Assuming that someone coming from a background as a full-time performer would be a better fit for me as a student than someone without similar name recognition would eliminate many accomplished teachers from consideration.

At any rate, although I was initially frustrated when my top two choices of studio teachers were unavailable, it was fortuitous that I would finally get the chance to work with Robert Harrison several years after my undergraduate trip to Boulder. We met in the mountains, but we finally connected in the Midwest.

2 Early Influences and Examples

The Importance of Curiosity, Mentors, and Role Models

Robert John Harrison was born on September 29, 1949, in the rural community of Dodgeville, Wisconsin, which had approximately 2,000 residents at the time. His father, Donald Carkeek Harrison, was drafted into the US Navy soon after his high school graduation and served during the Second World War. After returning home when the war ended, he held a variety of jobs throughout his life, all of which helped him provide the necessities for his family, though they did not allow for much in the way of extravagances. Bob's mother, Verda Jayne (Evans) Harrison, was no stranger to work, holding down two jobs while she attended high school in order to contribute financially, since her parents had lost their family farm following the Great Depression. Once she was married, Jayne spent time as a homemaker, raising Bob and his older brother, Bruce, before eventually returning to work as a clerk, first for a family-run bank and then at General Telephone.

Though neither Donald nor Jayne had the opportunity to attend college, they always emphasized the importance of education in the Harrison household and expected their children to take their studies seriously. That being said, Bob admits that the start of his academic life was, to say the least, humble. He knew exactly how much he was underachieving due to the example of an academic overachiever in his own house. "When I compared my intelligence, my capability to learn, to that of my brother, who is four years older than I am, we were quite different," Bob says. "He didn't have to crack a book. In high school, he was enrolled in the highest levels of math and science and just aced everything. In fact, he graduated as salutatorian of his graduating class. I was the opposite."

It wasn't that Bob's entire body of academic work was underwhelming, but he definitely had greater aptitude and interest in some areas while he generally achieved less in others. "My grades throughout high school were very poor. I think music was the only area where I acquired any As," he says. "But in the hard sciences, mathematics, courses like that, there was no way I could handle anything other than the introductory levels. Those courses were very difficult for me."

Therefore, when report card time came around, there were some uncomfortable conversations around the "supper table" ("We ate 'supper' in Wisconsin."). "I was always embarrassed to bring home my report cards to my parents," he says (Figure 2.1). "My father was the one who responded to those Ds. I can remember him very quietly offering his response. He never raised his voice, but he would look up over his plate and say, 'Well, you better get these grades up.' And occasionally, he would say, 'And if you don't, you're going to have a rough life.' I still remember that."

Even his musical studies, in which he tended to excel, revealed certain weaknesses. He became critically aware of these deficits after finishing high school. "I entered college, essentially, with no music theory skills," he says, "though they had been taught. The choral director and band director, who were very good, took me aside to help me. But at that time, I just didn't get it. They, with good intentions, were trying to teach me the circle of fifths and the concept of transposition of instruments. My reaction was simply, 'What? Why would a B-flat trumpeter read something in B-flat, when it's coming out of the frickin' horn in C?' That just frustrated the hell out of me," he says. "And, I must say, it still does."

Figure 2.1 Bob as a four-year-old, by photographer Edgar Obma, around 1953.

Despite his lack of understanding, he profusely credits the admirable efforts of his more-than-capable teachers throughout his education. "Still today, I have a tremendous amount of respect for those teachers. Their efforts should be noted," he says. "They did all they could to encourage me and to help me build my musical skills."

College provided a necessary wake-up call for Bob, which led him to adopt a new degree of academic discipline to take his musical skills to the next level. After graduating from Dodgeville High School in 1967, he enrolled at Milton College in nearby Milton, Wisconsin, eighty miles from his hometown. "Honestly," he admits, "I'm surprised that I was admitted into any school." A private, liberal arts college with an enrollment of fewer than 1,000 students, Milton eventually closed its doors in 1982. Its academic rigors, however, were tremendously challenging to Bob. "I was swamped there," he says. "I really wasn't reading music well. Yes, I knew the lines and spaces. But that was just about it."

Even in his nonmusic courses, he recalls his underwhelming performance, notably a D- in English Composition. "I wrote like I spoke," he explains. "Where I grew up, there wasn't always an agreement between a subject and a noun. That was the way I spoke, so I thought that was the way I should write." That course left an impression that has stuck with him ever since. "When I wrote my resignation letter at IU, it took me two days of editing and re-editing," he recalls. "Even then, I still never felt comfortable with it. It goes back to that D-, which was good for me."

He felt behind scholastically, in part because he could see how intelligently his peers could engage with the subject matter of their coursework. "I had classmates around me who could answer these incredible questions. And I felt like a fool," he says. "I was stunned and really in awe—not in so much fear, but in awe—of what my peers knew, and how quickly they could throw their hands up in the air to answer a question, which I had no possible way of answering."

Several emotions coursed through him at the time, intimidation and guilt primary among them. "I don't like intimidation any more than anybody else, and I'm not so sure that it is all that good as a teaching tool, to teach somebody through intimidation," he says. "Of course, I recognize that my professors weren't intimidating me. My peers weren't intimidating me. I had brought that on myself."

This self-realization was the spark that awakened in him a desire to match up. He desperately wanted to operate from the same base of knowledge and understanding that his classmates already seemed to possess. His solution? The sincerest form of flattery: imitation. "Silently, I started to emulate them. In order for me to become a good student, I had to understand how they got where they were."

Academic Awakening

In many ways, Bob and I had similar childhood experiences. From my perspective, all three of my siblings were academic overachievers and, although I know they worked hard at their studies, it just seemed to come easier to them than it did for me, at least in my mind. Looking back, that's perhaps an unfair assessment, but it was certainly my perception at the time. My dad also set the example for academic accomplishment in our household, having been a high school valedictorian, graduating from college with a history major, two minors (Spanish and philosophy), and a teaching certificate, studying in Europe for two years, and later earning a master's degree in guidance counseling while working a full-time job. He didn't subscribe to the "Just do your best" mentality many of our friends' parents adopted. In our house, the oft-repeated phrase was "Bust your butt to get that A!" I appreciate now that I was encouraged (expected) to aim for a tangible goal with my academics, which is something I probably needed at the time, given my overall lack of motivation when it came to schoolwork. This approach, however, ingrained the idea that the way to get the most out of a class was to get an A, which may or may not be true. Therefore, much of my effort in school prioritized earning good (or good enough) grades rather than developing an interest in, and curiosity about, the subject matter. Predictably, I tended to do well in subjects that came more easily to me (the arts and humanities) and I did poorly in subjects that were more of a challenge (math and science).

Bob and I both had an acute awareness of our early struggles as students. We also both knew how inadequate we felt when we compared ourselves to our bright siblings—and how those feelings were exacerbated if others pointed out that same disparity. Maybe that has caused us to, at times, undervalue our intelligence. Or, conversely, maybe we're the only ones who truly and fairly assess our own intellectual capacities. "I have thought about this a lot throughout my life," Bob says. "People say to me, 'You're so bright. You're so intelligent. You're so on top of things.' And I still say, 'Well, no, I'm really not.' I have the records to indicate that. It was easy to convince myself, not so much that I wasn't bright, but that somehow I didn't get it."

Just as Bob decided to emulate his classmates and their habits as a way to improve his own academic performance, I had an epiphany of my own in my academic journey as an undergraduate student. During my sophomore year, I took a philosophy class taught by Fr. Rene McGraw, a Benedictine priest and humanities professor. I had never heard such profound, mind-opening ideas as those that were presented and discussed in his course. In fact, I found it difficult to get through the assigned readings in time for class since, after every page or two, I would have to stop and ponder what I had just read. I tried to soak up all that Professor McGraw was saying while also sitting dumbstruck at the way many of my classmates could engage with the material, as evidenced by their comments in class discussions. In a way, I felt paralyzed by the conversations, since I truly believed I had nothing floating around in my head that would contribute anything of substance to what was being said.

I ended up with a C in the class, which, according to my previous beliefs, would have indicated a failure of sorts. I have no argument against the fact that my performance in the class was average, as reflected in the grade received. But just because I did not receive an A did not mean that I failed to learn and grow as a result of the class. Quite to the contrary, the course stands out as one of the best and most meaningful I have ever taken. By serving as a turning point in the way I approached my studies, it is likely that this single class had the greatest overall impact on my life in academia.

Another factor that I know increased the impact of the course for me was the individual attention Professor McGraw offered to his students. One time in particular, he stayed with me for an hour after class (at my request) to continue discussing philosophy and how it may practically influence our everyday life choices. This is the sort of academic nurturing I needed and, as a dedicated educator, he was more than happy to provide it. By no means were his students coddled. He held high standards for the class and had no qualms about giving me the C that truly reflected my performance that semester. I also never considered challenging the grade, lobbying Professor McGraw for something higher, or making last-minute requests for extra credit. This was partly because I knew he wouldn't change my grade, and partly because, for the first time, I really didn't care about my grade. I just wanted to engage with the material and to see his brain at work as he presented all sides of an issue when leading our discussions. And I wanted more opportunities to observe and imitate this outstanding educator.

Compelled to Listen

Bob also credits the individual mentoring he received as an undergraduate as key to his eventual academic success. The small class sizes at Milton College led to favorable student-to-teacher ratios, which Bob believes were crucial to the development of his skills and understanding.

One of the more formative experiences during his undergraduate years—and an example of the dedication of his professors—actually occurred outside the classroom. On occasion, Thomas F. Sanborn, the professor of piano, choral music, and conducting, would invite his colleagues on the music faculty, as well as a group of interested students, to his apartment in nearby Fort Atkinson, Wisconsin, for informal "listening parties." The evenings would start with a meal prepared by Sanborn (who was known for his culinary skills), after which everyone would gather around the record player with scores in hand to listen to a designated masterwork. Both Bob and his wife, Sandy (his classmate and girlfriend at the time), were often invited to attend. On one of the first occasions, Bob and Sandy were told to bring a score of Bach's *St. Matthew Passion*. "I didn't know what that was," Bob remembers. "But I wasn't going to say, 'What's that?' I had displayed enough stupidity in his class that I wasn't going to display any more, knowingly." So he went to the library and checked out a copy that he and Sandy could share. The particular recording he chose, which was a new release at the time, featured soloists Dietrich Fischer-Dieskau, Peter Pears, Elizabeth Schwarzkopf, Christa Ludwig, Nicolai Gedda, and Walter Berry, conducted by Otto Klemperer. "We had a lovely dinner, had good conversation, and then we turned ourselves around. We students, about six of us, sat on the floor, and we listened to the entire recording of *St. Matthew Passion*," Bob says. "There was no talking. There was no discussion. We sat and listened. It was an hours-long listening session. At the end of it, there was complete silence. Everyone was so moved. The students and the adults, as well. There was just complete silence."

Bob always appreciated the opportunity these listening sessions provided and the example those professors set. He recognizes that it was an early lesson in how to actively listen, by ending conversations, eliminating distractions, and giving full attention to a score and a recording. The sessions also inspired him to learn why these singers and these compositions were so valued by his mentors. "What did that do for me?" Bob asks. "I began to listen to Fischer-Dieskau. I began to listen to Ludwig. I began to listen to Schwarzkopf. I bought everything that Schwarzkopf recorded. I bought everything that Gedda recorded. And in doing so, it would provoke questions that I would take to my professors."

Before these listening sessions, Bob had another formative experience as an undergraduate student. In 1969, he and a few of his friends from the music department piled in his voice teacher Susan Blumer's Dodge Charger and took a road trip to Lawrence University in Appleton, Wisconsin—two hours north of Milton—to see the famed soprano Elizabeth Schwarzkopf in recital. At the time, he didn't even know who she was. "I only went because my teacher said we should go," he recalls. The impressions Schwarzkopf made on the young student began from the first moment she appeared on stage. "She walked out so gracefully and elegantly. As soon as you saw the toe of her shoe, when she made an entrance on the stage with pianist Geoffrey Parsons, that woman was in command. Wouldn't you love to go to a recital and see that?"

Besides the advantage such an aligned posture might provide to her singing, Bob was even more struck by the confidence and self-assuredness it conveyed. "She knew she was a hostess that night," he says. "She was hosting a feast of music. And by carrying herself the way she did, she put all of us in a state of complete comfort. You could sit in your chair and not be distracted from what was most important in her mind—these musical statements."

Every time this recital came up in our conversations, which it often did, it would lead to additional recalled memories, sidetracks, and tangents. With each retelling, Bob almost seemed to place himself back in the moment, though it was more than half a century ago, and would simply relive it and revel in how powerful an experience it was. Undoubtedly, part of what impacted him so strongly was that, even at the early stages of his musical education, when he was admittedly ignorant of so many aspects of artistry, so much of her performance made perfect sense to him. "When I heard Schwarzkopf that night . . . " he trails off before continuing, "Oh, my God. I didn't even know what the hell she was singing about. I couldn't speak a word of German. But, at the same time, I understood her message. She touched me. She reached me. I had a pretty good idea, when she sang *Verborgenheit* [by Hugo Wolf], what she was talking about. I come back to that moment often, thinking that she may have been the first important voice teacher I ever had, simply by my attendance at that concert."

His classmates who joined him at that recital responded much like they did after their first hearing of the *St. Matthew Passion*. "On the ride home from Lawrence to Milton, there was no discussion," he says. "Nobody could say anything. We were struck, and in a completely different place. There were no words for what we had just heard."

Bob remains a staunch Schwarzkopf enthusiast and still refers listeners to her recordings. "When I hear someone say, 'Oh, you have to hear that recording of Renée Fleming singing the *Four Last Songs* of Strauss,' I'll say, 'Fine. But now you should go listen to Schwarzkopf.'"

Piqued by the experience he had at the recital, Bob remembers going back to Professor Sanborn, who had hosted the listening parties, and asking, '"Why did you want us to listen to Schwarzkopf when you played the *St. Matthew Passion* for us?' He said, 'She's the greatest interpreter of words and music alive today.'"

Assessing Our Musical Idols

Schwarzkopf is certainly a renowned singer of her era, and many besides Bob hold high regard for her still today. Is she the greatest artist of her generation? Should she be looked to as an example to which singers should aspire? Perhaps. Of course, beauty is in the eye (and ear) of the beholder. Despite all that Bob admires in her artistry, he still acknowledges certain imperfections. For example, to his ears, she often seemed to struggle with intonation. This deficiency, however, didn't dampen his appreciation of all that she was doing well. "Elizabeth Schwarzkopf and Janet Baker are two singers I'll listen to without even caring if they are out of tune," he says. "If you're just listening to intonation they would drive you crazy because Schwarzkopf was often sharp and Baker could be sharp and flat. Who gives a flying whatever? They were great! They made a lot of money singing out of tune. And for that reason, people either liked them or hated them. But Schwarzkopf especially could lift words and music off the page like no other of her time. And how she delivered diction, how she delivered color to lift the poetry off the page, was something to behold. It just made you sit up in your chair." Obviously, in his list of priorities, a true commitment to the expression of the text outranked all other factors.

I never had the opportunity to hear Schwarzkopf in person—she retired from performing in 1979 and died in 2006—though I do own a few of her recordings, which I have recently listened to again. Unlike Bob, it is difficult for me to get past some of the intonation issues he has pointed out. Understanding that recording quality may be part of the issue, I also know that I could never fairly evaluate her abilities without hearing *and* seeing her in performance. Ultimately, it doesn't really matter that Bob and I have the same opinions on who the greatest artists are. This is a subjective art, after all. But I do take his opinions to heart. Knowing his admiration of her artistry, I give her recordings greater attention than I otherwise would.

I also have no doubt that some of his affection for Schwarzkopf comes from the fact that he was exposed to her singing at a crucial point in his development. If he were to hear the same recital performance today that he did all those years ago, he might have many of the same reactions as he did back then. He might also have additional criticisms that he didn't have the capacity to recognize back then. As mentioned earlier, the brain is notorious for misremembering events. In our interviews alone, Bob recounted the Schwarzkopf recital numerous times. Like the game of telephone, it seems likely that some inaccuracies may have unknowingly crept in over the decades with each retelling. Over time, the stories may have molded into the lessons he was intending to get across to his students rather than reflecting the actual events.

That being said, memories do tend to consolidate more deeply in our minds when they are accompanied by strong emotions—a phenomenon author and pedagogue Lynn Helding explores in her book *The Musician's Mind: Teaching, Learning, and Performance in the Age of Brain Science*. As Helding explains, when episodic memories (our memories of life experiences) contain strong emotion, such as the joy of one's wedding day or the grief experienced after the loss of a loved one, it "rockets an event from routine to remarkable in an instant."[1] Clearly, Bob was experiencing powerful emotions during and after that concert. Does this mean his recollections are more likely to be accurate? Perhaps. Again, who is to say?

All I know is that I have fond memories of my own that seem to live photogenically in my mind—idyllic childhood moments, perfect vacations, and even performances where nearly everything seemed to go exactly as planned. I cannot say with any certainty that I remember them accurately; they live only in the past and in my memory. Even so, the lessons and experiences I take from them are as real to me as they can be and, as such, they influence my life as I move forward. In the same vein, as an avid reader, some of the most influential people in my life are characters of fiction I have never met. There is much to be gained from the example of others, tasting the agony of life's more intense lessons without having to physically experience the circumstances ourselves (thankfully!). Therefore, I do not believe that an experience has to have actually happened to me for it to be "real" enough to have a powerful influence.

As it relates to Bob's devotion to Schwarzkopf, there are artists in my life whom I likely adore due to beloved memories. Because of the power of these memories, I may resist truly and objectively assessing their artistic capabilities. I do not believe, however, that this diminishes their importance or influence in my life as a singer and teacher. Schwarzkopf did not need to sing with pitch-perfect intonation for me to appreciate her influence on Bob, which has then, through educational succession, influenced me. As it is, whenever I hear a recording of Schwarzkopf, a woman I never met, never saw in live performance, and with whom I have no experiences tied to strong emotions, I think of Bob, my trusted mentor, and I keep listening.

Fathers and Sons

Naturally, Bob's upbringing had a significant influence on his adult years, and he looks back at it with gratitude. He was happy to share his successes with his parents when he could—a desire that hasn't truly dissipated even though both of his parents have passed away. "I wish that my late father was alive," Bob says, "because he would have felt very proud to know that I retired after an accomplished and successful career as an educator. Not that the salary or status of being a professor at a place like IU was the end-all, but he still would have been very proud. In his own way, he understood the value of higher education. He would tell my brother and me, 'I want you boys to go to college so that you have better lives than your mother and I have.' And yet, they were easily capable of providing for our needs. We always had a roof over our heads and food on our table. Though he could not go to college—he went immediately into the war—he understood the importance of higher education."

One accomplishment he was able to share with his parents was his graduation from the University of Arizona with a Doctor of Musical Arts degree. "I was 36 when I got my doctorate," he says, "so I was old enough to understand that this was quite a crossing point, quite an accomplishment. But I also wanted my parents to witness it. We had the money, fortunately, so Sandy and I flew them to Arizona. My father was exceptionally proud and moved by that. It was the first time I saw him cry. Sandy took a picture of me in my regalia standing with my two parents. I still have that picture in a shoebox somewhere. I just wish that he had been alive to witness and share in my other successes."

Emotional stoicism, especially a resistance to shedding tears, is typical among many Midwestern men of past generations—and probably still today. There was only one other time in Bob's life that he can recall seeing his father cry. "The day that I, with my mother's permission, moved my father into a nursing home was the day he left home for the last time and never returned," Bob says. "I stayed with him for the first night, but the next day I had to fly back to Colorado. He was in his bed and he was content, though his mind was very altered at that point in his life. I said, 'You know, Dad? I want to tell you before I go, so that you don't forget, that I love you.' And he replied, 'Bob, I love you.' That was the first time I told him that I loved him and the first time he said it to me. And that was the second time I saw him cry."

Volumes have been written about the relationships between fathers and sons, and I could certainly write my own. There are two photos of my own dad, Jerry, that have special meaning to me, partly because they so clearly display the influence he had on me. The first photo appeared on the front page of the *Anamosa Journal-Eureka*, the weekly newspaper serving our town of 3,500 people and the even smaller surrounding communities in the county (Figure 2.2). The issue is dated December 22, 1982. On the left-hand side of the paper is a picture from the Anamosa High School choir's December concert. The choir has a tradition at this concert of welcoming alumni and members of the community to come up on stage, find a spot on the risers, and join in the singing of the "Hallelujah Chorus" from Handel's *Messiah*. Perhaps it was a slow news week, but Dad is pictured singing with the choir, in the center of the front page of the newspaper, and is even mentioned by name in the caption. To the right of that picture is a second photo, this one taken at the Saint Patrick's Elementary School Christmas concert. There are several students in the photo, but there I am, front and center, my mouth open wide, singing my heart out with my classmates. What the photographer probably thought was a cute father-and-son moment to highlight for the newspaper also perfectly encapsulates the role my dad played in my life. Not only did he allow me to sing and encourage me to sing, he modeled it by unabashedly singing himself.

I've seen it written that the most influential person in a child's life is often the parent of the same gender. In hindsight, I can see how my small-town upbringing adhered to many stereotypical gender norms, some of which are more than a bit embarrassing to recall. But, in my life, that assessment of influence certainly holds true. Thankfully, the example he set of what it means to be a man reached beyond many of those norms. According to Dad, men should be gentle and kind. Men should have intellectual pursuits. Men can be spiritual and have a curiosity about life beyond the physical. And, despite the many messages I received from society, he taught me that men should sing.

The second photo of Dad requires some explanation. First of all, he is a man of many hats. And nearly all of those hats are Chicago Cubs baseball caps. Dad grew up an avid baseball fan. He started cheering for the Cubs early on, since the game broadcasts on static-heavy WGN AM radio reached all the

Figure 2.2 Front page of the *Anamosa Journal-Eureka*, December 22, 1982.

way from Chicago to their family farm in eastern Iowa. Dad had an illustrious high school baseball career, if he does say so himself, and he is particularly proud of how his ragtag team of rural kids from the local Catholic school once beat the team from the public high school. He continued to enjoy the sport by coaching my siblings and me in our softball and baseball teams at various levels throughout our childhood. Now in his 80s, not too many family gatherings go by without him retelling the story of the team of fourteen-year-olds he once coached to a tournament championship by beating not one, but two rival teams known for their outstanding baseball programs.

Throughout our childhood, Dad owned a series of Cubs caps—the traditional all-blue cap with the red "C" in front—each of which had a dedicated role. His oldest cap was the most ragged and worn. This was the one he wore when painting the house, spraying his fruit trees with insecticide, or mowing the lawn. There was a mid-grade cap (not new, but nowhere near the rough condition of the house-painting cap) that was for more everyday use. He wore this cap when walking around the yard "watching the trees grow," sitting on the porch during a summer rain, or when coaching one of our teams (the other coaches wore caps with our team's logo—our dad always wore a Cubs cap). Then there was his newer, "dressy" Cubs cap that he wore on nicer occasions like family reunions, town parades and festivals, or on family trips. Eventually, when he found a good deal, he bought a newer Cubs hat and every other hat would be demoted one rung on the ladder.

When I was a junior in high school, the booster club for our school's athletics department held a fundraiser. My brother, Jeremy, and I were both heavily involved in school sports, and Mom and Dad attended nearly every game, match, and meet—home or away, 92 degrees and humid or 29 degrees and snowing. Dad donated to the fundraiser, for which he was given a cap with our team name, "Raiders," written across the front. My siblings and I thought it was funny that he brought home this cap since we couldn't really imagine him wearing anything other than a Cubs cap. Sure enough, the Raiders cap found a home on the top shelf of his closet, next to the rotation of Cubs caps. I chided him about it once, teasingly explaining that most fans wear the logos of the teams they are rooting for when they go to games as a way of showing support. He reacted with, "Oh, is that right?" which is the trademark phrase he offers to my siblings and me when he wants to acknowledge something we have said without agreeing with us. I didn't give the cap another thought after that.

Each year, the last home football game of the high school season is designated as "Parent's Night." All the student athletes line up on one side of the field and all their parents line up on the other. One by one, we approached the 50-yard line as the announcer introduced each athlete and the athlete's parents. We were all given a flower to present to our parents, then we posed for a photo, after which the parents headed to their seats and the athletes ran off for pregame warmups. On Parent's Night of my junior year, as I approached midfield, I could see Mom sensibly dressed for the cold late fall evening in a winter coat and snow pants to stay warm in the stands. Dad wore his winter

Figure 2.3 Brian with his parents, Jerry and Carolyn, 1991.

coat, as well, but instead of his dressy Cubs cap, he was wearing the Raiders cap, to support the team and to support his son—a seemingly small gesture that meant a thousand words to me (Figure 2.3).

Fathers and sons. Bob and I could both write volumes. I'm not sure we ever outgrow the desire to make them proud or ever forget the lessons they taught us. It was nothing short of life-changing that mine encouraged me to sing.

Note

1 Lynn Helding, *The Musician's Mind: Teaching, Learning, and Performance in the Age of Brain Science* (Lanham, MD: Rowman & Littlefield Publishing Group, Inc.), 75.

3 Professional Life

First Jobs, Dealing with Rejection, and Personal Sacrifice for Professional Gain

In stark contrast to how Bob's college experience began, he ended his time at Milton College with an abundance of confidence. As his musical understanding and skills developed over those years, and with his bachelor's degree newly in hand, he was feeling good about taking the next step in his career. Having been a big-fish talent in every small Wisconsin pond in which he had thus far swum, he felt certain his trajectory of success would continue. Bob states it more bluntly: "I was pretty full of myself," he says. "I was sent off to New York City with the idea that I was going to set the place on fire."

In the summer of 1971, he packed up his hard-sided Samsonite suitcase ("It probably weighed 50 pounds when it was empty.") and headed off for the Big Apple. Professor Sanborn had a connection in New York City with two singers who had been regular choristers in the Robert Shaw Chorale, Marlys Trunkhill and her husband, William Wiederanders. They generously offered to let Bob stay with them in their apartment on West 103rd Street while he got settled in the city.

In his initial weeks, he sat in on rehearsals with the choral ensembles his hosts were involved with, observed a professional recording session with the Clarion Orchestra, and even had an audition with Thomas Pyle ("Shaw's right-hand man"), which led to some of his first singing engagements.

Unsurprisingly, things did not come quite as easily as he thought they would. The competition for vocal employment was fierce and nothing like he had previously experienced. "I always regard New York City as my finishing school, meaning, it finished me," he says. "It taught me some humility. It did not take me long to realize that I was easily outsung by many, which caused some panic and some wonder of, 'Is this the place I should be? Am I here too early?' But nonetheless, the work was generous."

As a freelance chorister, he had many formative experiences, singing under the direction of notable conductors like Robert Shaw, Leopold Stokowski, Eve Queler, Gregg Smith, and Dave Brubeck. "I was in the chorus when [Leonard] Bernstein did his 1,000th performance with the New York Philharmonic," he says. "It was a gala and, interestingly enough, [his future IU colleague] Martina Arroyo was the soloist in Mahler's Second Symphony. It's little things like that that this little kid from Wisconsin got to do. I just shouldn't have gotten where I got."

Like many New York City musicians, Bob also had a day job, working for Uris Building Corporation as a mail clerk, operating their behemoth of a Xerox machine. Eventually, he was offered a promotion within the company that would provide a steady salary, paid vacation, and health insurance. This offer coincided with a precipitous drop in funding for New York-based arts

Figure 3.1 Bettina Bjorksten, Bob's voice teacher at the University of Wisconsin-Madison, in a 1953 photo. Courtesy of the Wisconsin Historical Society, WHI-83605.

organizations, making singing jobs less plentiful than when he first arrived. This convergence caused some soul-searching. "Sandy and I sat down with a yellow legal pad," he says. "We had two columns: Why should I stay in music? Why should I not?" They eventually decided, after five years in New York City, that it was time to move home to Wisconsin.

Part of what was calling him back to the Midwest was the opportunity to begin his master's degree at the University of Wisconsin-Madison. In particular, he wanted to work with the German soprano and voice teacher Bettina Bjorksten (1908–2012) (Figure 3.1). Born in Frankfurt-am-Main, Germany, she came to Madison with quite an educational lineage. Bjorksten had studied with German soprano Ria Ginster and with Émile Jacques-Dalcroze, the Swiss composer and music educator who developed the Dalcroze eurhythmics pedagogical approach. The influence of Dalcroze was not the only lineage Bjorksten brought to her teaching. As a young child, she had studied in Germany with Maria Montessori, the namesake of the thousands of Montessori schools worldwide that adhere to the philosophy of education she founded. Since her mother was an accomplished pianist, Bjorksten's family also frequently hosted well-known musicians, including members of the Budapest String Quartet and composers Alban Berg and Paul Hindemith.

It is difficult for Bob to articulate exactly what it was that drew him to Bjorksten when he was just twenty-eight years old. It may have been her reputation for seriousness that attracted him since he had a desire to incorporate greater discipline into his practice and studies. Regardless, he readily acknowledges the impact she had on his musical development. "She was probably my greatest influence," he says. "She taught me the importance of being an intelligent musician."

Bob also credits Bjorksten as being the first to encourage him to become a teacher. Before his second year at the University of Wisconsin, a teaching assistantship became available, which Bjorksten offered to him. He initially turned the offer down. Since he was not in need of the financial aid and stipend it would provide, he felt it should go to someone else. Bjorksten intervened. "She said, 'I want you to have the privilege of teaching,'" he recalls. "That's what set me in motion—full speed—to teach. I enjoyed it immensely and decided that's what I wanted to do."

Bob graduated with his master's degree in 1978, which aligned with Bjorksten's mandated retirement at age seventy. As the following school year approached, a former student of Bjorksten reached out to her about a one-year teaching position that had opened up at the University of Wisconsin-Oshkosh. Bob says, "She called Bettina and said, 'Do you have anybody?' She said, 'I do.' So they hired me." In addition to voice lessons, the position involved teaching a voice class and a vocal literature course and conducting a women's chorus. "That was fun," he says. "It allowed me to buy my first and only baton."

Two other one-year appointments followed. Bob spent the 1979–80 school year teaching at Wichita State University in Kansas and then 1980–1 at the University of Arkansas in Fayetteville. Then, in 1981, he was hired as an assistant professor at the University of Colorado Boulder.

It's difficult to say where Bob's career would have gone had Bjorksten not recommended him for that first job in Oshkosh. He recalls sending out about forty job applications for college teaching positions in the spring and summer of 1978. He was rejected for every one of them. Although most of the "Thanks, but no thanks" notifications came in the form of mimeographed postcards, Robert Fink, chair of the search committee at Western Michigan University, took the time to send an actual, personalized letter. Bob was so struck by the kindness of the gesture that he kept the letter, even though it was a rejection. When Bob later accepted the position at the University of Colorado, Fink himself had also accepted a position at CU as the dean of the College of Music. "After I'd signed on the dotted line with the University of Colorado, my first semester, I took the rejection letter in to Dean Fink," Bob says. "I jokingly said to him, 'See what you wrote? See how unkind you were?'"

A Resume of Failures

I have some letters of rejection of my own. An entire box, actually. I initially started keeping them as a way to keep track of which jobs I had applied to. As the pile grew, it was probably a bit masochistic to continue keeping them. But, at this point in my life, it's an intriguing record of what might have been, as well as a reminder to stay humble, knowing how often I was turned down.

A few years ago, there was a thread on one of the voice teacher groups I follow on social media that caught my attention. One of the moderators, Ian Howell, posted about how nearly every successful performer has to endure a series of failures and rejections before becoming established in the industry. But, because we only know them for their achievements, we assume they never had to struggle. In some cases, their previous failed attempts are intentionally hidden and unacknowledged, as though they were simply born into stardom. This can be discouraging for aspiring performers who may hope to learn from their examples. Rather than leaving a trail of breadcrumbs that others might follow to similar success, these performers cover their tracks so others won't know how they became so accomplished.

Howell then asked if any of us would be willing to share some of the failures we've encountered over the years. He offered his own experiences first by describing disastrous auditions, being rejected by agents, not getting rehired by companies he had previously performed with, and on and on. Even so, he had an international singing career, became a voice teacher at two leading conservatories, and now directs the Embodied Music Lab, which he founded.[1] His many failures occurred before, during, and after his biggest successes.

Another person in the group, Yvonne Gonzales Redman, posted about how difficult it was to stay financially afloat when she was trying to start her career. Considering how much money she was spending on voice lessons, coachings, audition wear, headshots, and so on, she said she went to so many auditions where the only positive takeaway was that her backpack was lighter due to emptying out her wallet. She later went on to an eighteen-year career singing at the Metropolitan Opera and is now a professor of voice and vocal pedagogy at the University of Illinois School of Music.

Lots of others were jumping in with their own lists of failures, so I posted as well. I had to go back to my "box of rejections" to count up the letters but, as it turns out, I have applied for more than 100 university teaching positions over the years. I was named a finalist for ten of those jobs and was invited to those campuses for in-person interviews. Those ten interviews resulted in only one job offer, which I turned down due to the salary offer, which was significantly lower than I was expecting (and lower than what I was already earning in my high school teaching job). The numbers don't lie—in 99 percent of those jobs, I was not the person the committees wanted. That's a lot of rejection. Of course, each one was difficult to take at the time (ranging from disappointing to devastating). I suppose at any point I could have taken the not-so-subtle hint that I should try my hand at another profession, but I guess I was just determined enough (and had been encouraged enough by others) to keep at it.

The irony is, had I been offered and then accepted any of those other jobs—which I would have been happy to do at the time—it would have pulled me off the path that has led me to where I am now. And, although there is no "perfect" job, I quite enjoy and am tremendously grateful for the work I get to do every day in the place where I have landed. It's certainly possible that one of those other jobs would have been a better fit for me than where I am now, or could still be in the future. But, I'd also like to think that I have an additional sense of appreciation for what I get to do in my career, especially knowing that it was not easily attained.

Right Place, Right Time

Of course, Bob recognizes that his career was built on solid education, hard work, and deep listening, but there was also a bit of good fortune in the mix. If Bjorksten had not recommended him for the job at UW-Oshkosh, he may not have had the experience necessary to be hired at the next job or the one after that. "I wouldn't have gotten where I got as a teacher had it not been for being in the right place at the right time," Bob acknowledges, "and I think that right place for me occurred when I got to Wichita State University." It was there that the seeds were planted for his hiring at the University of Colorado, which led to Indiana University. First of all, WSU faculty member Dorothy Crumb had studied with Berton Coffin, who was a CU Professor of Music and Chair of the Division of Voice for more than thirty years. Second, Dennis Jackson was the head of the search committee for the position Bob was hired for at CU. Jackson happens to be a WSU alum (who studied with the same voice teacher, Arthur Newman, as notable WSU alum and operatic superstar Samuel Ramey). "When my dossier surfaced at the University of Colorado Boulder, they then could call to speak with people at Wichita. That's being in the right place at the right time," Bob says. "The first full-time position is always the most difficult one to get—not that it's always easy to keep it."

In order to keep his position at CU over the long term, it was stipulated that he must earn a terminal degree before he would be considered for tenure. Therefore, after teaching for three years, Bob took a leave from Boulder in order to work on his Doctor of Musical Arts degree at the University of Arizona as a full-time student. However, he had serious misgivings about the endeavor. "I never thought I was smart enough to get a doctorate," he says. "I was scared to death of it."

A few of his courses seemed to justify that fear. Musicologist James Anthony, in particular, had a reputation for holding his students to what seemed like impossibly high standards for academic work. The author of numerous articles on French Baroque music in *The New Grove Dictionary of Music and Musicians*, he was "uncompromising," as Bob says, in his expectations. "I still have a copy of Jim Anthony's exam that he gave to me for my comprehensive exams. And I still have some of my homework that I did with him, because a couple of them have an A+ on them. To get an A+ from Jim Anthony . . . " he trails off. "I've got that exam, and it is a doozy."

He had similar anxieties about other elements of his studies during the DMA program. "I feared my doctoral oral exams," he says. "For two years, I devoted at least one hour every day to studying for it, because I just couldn't allow myself to be thought too much of a fool. I just couldn't handle that."

Unlike some of his previous experiences in academia, this time he was ready for the challenge. "I surprised myself that I could do the work. I could do the music theory, I could do the musicology. I'm very proud of that, because that was not work I was capable of doing when I went to undergraduate school," he says. "It was probably the two greatest years of study I ever spent. It was a joy."

The coursework was set up in such a way that he knew he could complete the degree in two years, including one summer, as long as he passed the courses. "And Sandy was very generous because she taught general music those two years," he adds. "Bless her heart, she got teaching positions every time we moved."

Bob finished the degree in 1986, right on track—a Doctor of Musical Arts in Vocal Performance with a minor in Musicology. He, Sandy, and their three-year-old daughter, Joanna, then returned to Boulder, where he was awarded tenure in 1995 and full professorship in 2003.

Boulder to Bloomington

The time came, however, in the early 2000s when Bob started to wonder if his retirement should be closer rather than further away. He had already been teaching for twenty-five years and felt he perhaps had done all he could do in the field. Sandy was also reaching her own retirement. After another couple of years of teaching, she could retire from the public school system with her full pension and benefits. Bob was considering taking his own early retirement at the same time as Sandy, which gradually became the plan forward.

Then, in December of 2003, he received a call that caused him to reconsider. It was from Paul Kiesgen, Professor of Voice at the Indiana University School of Music (it became the Jacobs School of Music in 2005). Kiesgen informed Bob of an open position on the voice faculty at IU and inquired as to his potential interest in the position. That encouragement was all he needed. "I never thought twice about it," he says. "I applied."

Bob knew IU's reputation for hiring accomplished performers to serve on their teaching faculty. If that were to be the primary criterion for his hiring, he knew he would quickly be out of the running. It wasn't that his performance credits were insignificant. Quite the contrary. But he had never pursued a full-time career as a performer after leaving New York City. He had never appeared on the stage of the Metropolitan Opera or of any major opera company, as have many of IU's most well-known faculty throughout the years.

Bob did have colleagues and connections in the highest levels of the performance world, however. He had developed a cherished relationship with Dutch soprano Elly Ameling that started when she made recital appearances at CU. She agreed to write a letter of recommendation on his behalf for the position at IU. So did famed mezzo-soprano Frederica von Stade. He was humbled by their words of support and is convinced their influence made a difference with the search committee.

Of course, as often happens in faculty searches, a significant amount of time passed between Bob's submission of his application and any notification from those in charge. It wasn't until April that Bob finally received a second call from Kiesgen, who was chair of the search committee. He informed Bob that he was one of the top candidates for the position and indicated the committee's interest in scheduling a phone interview. After the phone interview, he was invited to an on-campus interview, after which he received positive feedback from the committee. One member in particular, Andreas Poulimenos, said to him, "We are so impressed with your work. My only fear is that you won't take the job. Will you take this job if it's offered?" Bob jokingly responded, "I probably will, just to irritate you."

Bob went home encouraged, expecting to hear back somewhat quickly since the process was fully underway. Several days passed, however, with no word from the committee. In thinking about this period of waiting, he recalls something his future IU colleague Gary Arvin would later say to him: "You know, Bob, Indiana is a big machine. It takes a long time for her to do a full crank."

After more than two weeks, and with nothing to lose, he decided to email Kiesgen to inquire about the status of the search and to ask if they had moved on to another, more preferred candidate. "Oh, no," Kiesgen told him. "The recommendation has already been made to the dean. You're the one." It was later that night that Bob received the call from Dean Gwyn Richards, praising his qualifications and offering him the job.

The initial offer did require some negotiation. The timing of the opening at Indiana was right for where Bob was in his career, but it was not exactly ideal for the Harrison family. As mentioned, Sandy was still two years away from retiring from her teaching position with full benefits. And their youngest daughter, Liliana, was about to enter her junior year of high school and was less than enthused about the prospect of moving to a new school in a new state for her last two years.

Therefore, Bob asked for an additional stipend beyond his salary so he could spend his first two years traveling between Boulder and Bloomington. After that two-year period, he committed to move to Indiana. This request was initially met with some resistance, with Richards pointing out that the IU faculty is a resident faculty. In response, Bob highlighted the concert touring schedules of some of the more prominent faculty members who were also considered part of that "resident faculty," a few of whom were undoubtedly on the road more days than they were on campus.

He also had one additional request: to join IU at the same rank he had earned at CU—full professorship with tenure. The initial offer was for a tenure-line position at the rank of assistant professor. Bob was clear that he would not accept the position if his previously awarded tenure was not recognized.

He felt comfortable making these requests for a few reasons. First, the committee members had told him during the on-campus interview that they were intentionally seeking a proven teacher, as opposed to someone coming from the performing ranks who had less teaching experience. That assured him that he would likely not be in competition with candidates who had the kind of high-level performing experience that was simply absent on his own resume. Therefore, he didn't have to pretend to be someone he wasn't, and he could stand on his record and lifelong career as a successful teacher. Secondly, he didn't *need* the job. He knew that he could simply stay put and finish his last two years at CU before retiring with Sandy. Certainly, that choice would involve much less trouble and upheaval at that stage in his life and career.

Richards went back to the committee with Bob's requests, including a counteroffer to the initial salary request. The next day he called Bob with an updated offer that included an increase in salary, a travel stipend, and full professorship. Thus began the accumulation of frequent flyer miles between the international airports of Denver and Indianapolis.

Bob later learned that he was not, in fact, the top choice of the committee. Apparently, the leading candidate remained at her current school, causing them to move on to him, their second choice. Ironically, the same thing happened to Bob before he was hired at CU. That committee's top candidate also turned the job down, leading them to extend an offer to Bob. He doesn't read too much into that, however, considering that he was, yet again, in the right place at the right time. "I was always second fiddle," he says. "Not a bad place to play, I guess."

On the Road. Again.

Bob did not look forward to the prospect of commuting every weekend for two years. But it was a sacrifice he was willing to make to be able to take advantage of this new opportunity. As for commuting, this was something else Bob and I had in common when we started our time in Bloomington.

When I was accepted into the doctoral program at IU in 2004, Erika and I had been married for five years and were living in northern Indiana. In order to make my return to school financially viable, we decided the best way for me to work toward the degree would be to commute. That would allow Erika to continue working in her field and keep our family afloat financially, and for me to keep earning some income by continuing to work my weekend job as a music director at an area church. This decision meant that each Sunday afternoon, after the last of my three church services ended, we got to work doing laundry and cooking meals that we would then load into the car before I made the 200-mile, four-hour trip to an apartment in Bloomington, within walking distance of the IU campus. Once there, I would attend all my classes, practice my singing, and stay in the library until closing time in an effort to complete as much of my homework as possible before the weekend. Then, on late Friday afternoons after class, I would drive home to teach a handful of voice lessons, work my church music job, catch up on homework that wasn't completed during the week, and reacquaint myself with Erika. Once Sunday afternoon came around, the whole process would start over again.

By commuting, I was able to complete all my coursework in a relatively short amount of time (two years, including both summers). Since I was a non-scholarship student, the fact that we both could continue to work at our jobs meant that our long-term financial burden was significantly lower than if I had quit my job and paid for my education primarily through loans. Although it was a difficult stretch—and, admittedly, not the ideal way to do a degree—we knew it was a temporary situation that would hopefully set our household up for greater options in the future. Erika also knew how much I wanted to pursue doctoral studies, and the opportunity to attend a school like IU was too good to pass up. So Bob and I are both, quite literally, indebted to our wives for keeping our families out of debt while we were earning our final degrees. As such, all successes we have had that hinged on earning the terminal degree are truly accomplishments we share with our partners.

Obviously, Erika and I never wanted to spend most of two years apart. We had decided early on in our relationship that our commitment to each other would supersede our relationship to our careers and that, in building a life together, we should prioritize actually being together (Figure 3.2). Of course, other couples manage distance-based relationships successfully as they build their own formulas for how to navigate their marriages. Erika's mother reminded us once that her own father's job required him to be on the road Monday through Friday. For the majority of her parents' marriage, they spent the workweek apart, only seeing each other on weekends and vacations. Clearly, there are many paths.

Erika and I also recognize the tremendous privilege in our lives that continues to allow us to make the choice to be together rather than distanced. Not every couple has that option available to them. Still, over the years, it has meant making choices that, career-wise, might be better for one of us than for the other. For instance, after I finished my master's degree, at a point when many of my classmates were moving on to summer programs or year-long apprenticeships, or moving to big cities with the dreams of launching their performing careers, we chose to pursue Erika's career interests. This

Figure 3.2 Brian and Erika in front of the Bess Meshulam Simon Music Library and Recital Center at IU after the successful defense of his final doctoral project, May 2009.

involved moves to smaller communities where she could find work in her field (broadcast journalism). With each move, I had to do a bit of reinventing myself. Although I was always able to find jobs and opportunities in music, sometimes those jobs were more peripheral to music or had a focus that was not in my main area of interest. Nonetheless, in each of those jobs, I earned valuable skills and experience that apply directly to the work I am doing now.

As the months progressed, my heart ached a bit more each time we loaded up our Oldsmobile Cutlass Ciera, preparing to spend another week apart. Even so, my spirits always picked up when I saw the Indiana University exit signs, reminding me of the dream I was pursuing.

The fact that Bob was willing to make a similar sacrifice at a much later stage in his life, to follow his own Indiana University dream, was also inspiring to me. It reminds me that we always have to be open to change, both the welcome and unwelcome kind. My dad had a wonderful career working in the same building for thirty-four years. The younger version of me assumed that sort of stability was the mark of a successful career. To see someone like Bob move to a new job in a new state in a late-career stage was something I hadn't considered might ever be a part of my life. It may not be, but I know the possibility is there, and I have people like Bob in my life who have done just that whom I can look to as inspiration.

Like me, Bob also admits that he would not have engaged in a long-distance situation for the long term. "By the time I got to the second year," he says, "I had really grown tired of it." I don't know if either of us would have agreed to a similar arrangement if it would have been for four years, or even three. I suppose every couple has to work that out for themselves. But those two years also gave Erika and me a deeper appreciation of what it means to share your life with someone—year after year and, especially, day by day.

Note

1 The Embodied Music Lab is based in Ann Arbor, Michigan, and was founded in 2022. https://www.embodiedmusiclab.com/.

Part II
Lessons, Philosophies, and Practices

4 Embracing Eccentricities

"Sometimes, to make a point, you have to make a circus."

I have to believe that everyone who meets Bob is struck by his eccentricities. As mentioned previously, he has a variety of eye-catching eyeglasses, each pair a bit louder than the last. He sometimes told stories of visiting the specialty eyewear shop in Manhattan where he acquired most of these treasures. The shopkeeper knew him by name. If the eyes are the windows to the soul, Bob's soul is always adorned with the most spectacular window dressings.

Those who felt his eyeglasses were a bold statement needed only to walk into his studio to see just how high the bar could be raised. Bob's studio on the third floor of the Music Annex at IU ("the round building") was adorned with beautiful mid-century modern art glass vases and sculptures he had collected over the years, leading him to refer to his room as "the studio of glass and class."

His speaking voice is also an unmistakable characteristic—more identifiable than his fingerprints, I suspect. His prosody is wildly varied, from his high-pitched exclamations to his raucous, bombastic laugh. I remember a notable demonstration of the latter at a dress rehearsal of one of our university opera productions. Students and faculty were both allowed to attend these rehearsals, with the faculty sitting in the orchestra level and the students sitting in the balcony. After the rehearsal of this comedic opera, one of my classmates commented to Bob that she could hear his laughter all the way up in the upper balcony where she was sitting. He responded, with a wink, "Well, you know, I'm trained to project."

Bob also has an affinity for fancy shoes and socks. I remember the stack of shoeboxes piled along one of the walls in his studio. He would select an appropriate pair once he arrived for the day of teaching, which would be decidedly more ornate than the functional footwear that carried him across campus, trudging through Bloomington's four-season weather. In one conversation about his extensive shoe collection, I told him that he would probably be shocked to learn that my own shoe collection consisted of one pair of brown shoes, one pair of black shoes, one pair of sandals, and one pair of running shoes. He looked down at my feet, which were sporting the brown pair that day. Then he looked back up in mock disgust and said, "And just look at how scuffed they are!" I hadn't noticed.

When I encounter similar larger-than-life personalities who take such pleasure in out-of-the-ordinary things (Figure 4.1), I often wonder about the origin of

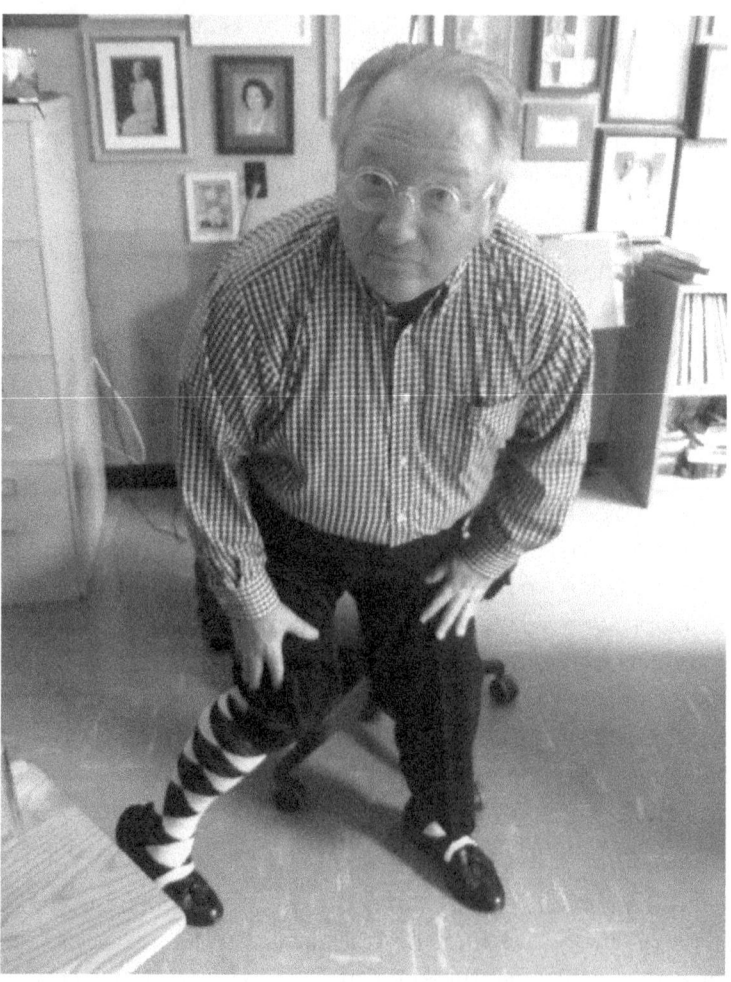

Figure 4.1 Bob's eccentricities include an affinity for fancy glasses, socks, and shoes. Photo courtesy of Bob's former student Olivia Savage, September 2012.

their eccentricities. When and why did he become a connoisseur of glasses, vases, and shoes? Does he really enjoy them as much as he seems to, or is it just for show? Similarly, is his loud-voiced, quick-to-laugh personality a true reflection of who he is, or is he playing a character? I can't jump inside the man's head to know for certain, but I absolutely believe he is authentically, unapologetically who he is. To my observation, he has long grown past the desire to put on airs or to live his life in any way other than being true to who he is. There is no hidden agenda with Bob. He does not expect everyone to share his interests or passions, but he is insistently himself, which is worthy of admiration if for no other reason than it is so rarely encountered in this age of social media posturing.

That being said, I also suspect that there is a deeper pedagogical purpose at play—one that is actually quite savvy. Bob admitted in one of our conversations, almost offhandedly, "One of the important elements of teaching is that sometimes, to make a point, you have to make a circus. What you are instructing sticks when it's attached to something just incredibly ridiculous."

Bob's wife, Sandy, was a devoted and accomplished public school teacher for thirty-one years, and she would often comment to him about how teaching really is a performance. Bob agrees, saying, "You're constantly performing. And the basis of that performance is hopefully to share the truth."

So perhaps some of his outrageousness was to aid the learning process. Once again, cognitive science has demonstrated that memories are more deeply ingrained when they are accompanied by strong emotions. We often think first of pain and trauma being the culprits of certain long-held memories. But laughter and amusement are signs of strong emotions, as well, and may also successfully embed certain lessons into our minds.

There may have been another motive for Bob's outrageousness. He was constantly asking students to bring more of themselves to the music they were performing and to take greater, more personal, often uncomfortable risks as creative interpreters. He wanted us to be courageous enough to bring the fullness of who we are to the work we were presenting. Perhaps it's arrogant to think that I could add anything to, for instance, a Schubert song that has been performed by many of the world's great singers over centuries. But, in another sense, I *have* to believe that I have something unique to contribute as a performer. If I don't believe it about myself, why would I expect an audience to want to listen to me? In this way, Bob led by example. He was already living out loud, in the shining fullness of his own being, for all to see. Knowing that he was so unapologetically himself, we were also free to unmute our own brilliance, refusing to hide our own light under the proverbial bushel basket.

Therefore, it makes perfect sense that the two characteristics Bob looked for in prospective students were curiosity and a penchant for being a little weird. "Students always had to demonstrate curiosity," he says. "Because if you don't have any curiosity, you aren't going to do anything for yourself. The weirder the curiosity, the more interest I had in a student. I wanted the weirdest people to work with—what others deemed weird. Why do you wear your glasses on the back of your head? Give me that kid."

I'm guessing that most of the graduates of the Harrison Studio are like myself in that we were unaware of this particular measuring stick. I suppose we should take it as a compliment that, upon evaluation, Bob determined that we were all weird enough to fit in.

From the Known to the Unknown

When Bob and Sandy were dating, as undergraduate classmates one year apart, Bob would often attend her music education classes with her when he didn't have a class of his own. One class period, Bob picked up a lesson that would become foundational to his educational philosophy. In a teaching methods course for junior high music students, the professor said, "When teaching, you must go from the known to the unknown." The takeaway for Bob was that, in order for a teacher to effectively transfer a piece of information to a student, the teacher has to connect it to a piece of information or relative piece of information that the student already understands—starting with what is familiar and using that as a bridge to a new concept. "That's what Professor Bernie Westland said in that class," Bob remembers. "I walked away and it stuck with me. That made teaching easy."

From that moment forward, Bob would always look for what students could identify with in order to "find ways of moving information from my head to the students' heads" by tying it to something they understand. "That was a constant part of my teaching every day," he says. "If you do not understand something, I will try to find another 'known' to share with you."

5 Learning via the Senses
Developing a Detail-Oriented Mind

One of the quickest ways for something to become "known" for Bob is to experience it through his senses. Throughout his life, his senses could easily pull his attention away from any task at hand—a quality that he admits made him a challenge to teach in the traditional classroom setting. On the other hand, it also likely contributed to his development as an artist. "If I heard something, felt something, tasted something, listened to something, smelled something, I was on it. If I heard some sound while I was in a classroom as a young child, it would sweep me away from the work that I was to be doing," he says. "It would capture me and hold me as a prisoner to it. If I saw something, maybe outside of the school window, or heard something outside or inside, if I picked something up from within my messy desk and it interested me, tactilely, I would be misdirected and I would literally give up what I was doing, even if I were taking an exam, or doing some kind of a worksheet that the teacher had handed out. I would be distracted from that and become engaged in what I was listening to or seeing or touching."

The trait of following his senses continued into his high school studies, where the sights and sounds of his musical experiences made him come alive in ways his other courses simply could not. "In high school, I had music for about an hour or an hour and a half each day through chorus. That was my only musical outlet, besides church choir," he says. "It was a great experience as I found myself being stimulated by sound. It didn't matter what period of music we were singing. I heard the music and it stimulated my body, it stimulated my brain, and it forced my body to want to move. I just responded with extreme excitement."

This phenomenon of having his attention completely enveloped by his senses has remained with him throughout the years. "Even today, if I see something or hear something—and it can be the most unimportant detail to others—I'll say, 'Sandy, listen to this!' or 'Look at this!' And she'll look at me like, 'What?'

Even as we're speaking now, I'm looking out at the drifts of snow outside my window and they're captivating to see. I can even see the footprints of the dog. How insignificant, but it captures my eyes."

This trait has led to some consternation in his household—his own and that of his family members. "If I'm engaged sensory-wise, in any way, and someone tries to talk to me, I can get upset. If I hear, taste, or feel something that's very important to me, though insignificant to someone else, I don't want to be distracted," he says. On occasion, he will bring up a topic to his wife or to one of his daughters only to be told that they had already talked with him about that in a previous conversation. "I'll say, 'Oh, you did? When?' And they'll say, 'Well, you must have had something on your mind.'"

Although this characteristic caused some problems as he was growing up—and he admits that it can still make him difficult to live with at times—Bob also acknowledges that these traits have likely contributed to his professional success in music. "Though it could easily distract me from my classwork in school, and I was often admonished for that by my father, it probably made me a very good student when learning music," he says.

Specifically, he has always been able to focus—perhaps fixate—on details in music. He sees and hears things that might go unnoticed by many. In our lessons together, he constantly pointed out details within the music that I simply hadn't noticed, or asked questions about the music that I had not thought to consider. In many of those cases, it seemed to me that he was simply thinking out loud, discussing what his attention was drawn to. In turn, this caused me to start expanding my attention to notice things that might otherwise pass me by. Sometimes, when listening to a piece of music, I would even think, "What would Dr. Harrison be hearing?" as if filtering my listening through his ears.

Attention to Detail

To be sure, there is a detail-oriented side to my personality, as well, even if it isn't my default way of thinking. And I know exactly where it comes from.

I remember one time when I was riding in the car through rural Iowa with my parents. My mother, Carolyn, was in the passenger seat and was taking in the farmland scenery that surrounded us—as beautifully pastoral as those reflected in so many Grant Wood paintings. At one point, while looking out the window, she said, "Look at that corn!" Dad responded in his typical fashion, as if pulled out of his own thoughts, with "Hmm?" She then began to elaborate. "Well, look at how short it is for this time of year. I suppose that's because of the heavy rains we got in the spring, so the farmers probably couldn't do their planting as early as usual and now the crops are behind where they should be for this time in the season. But all that rain must have prepped the soil well because the corn still looks really healthy—not like when it's short because of the lack of rain in a dry year. If it keeps up like this, we may not be eating corn on the cob until September, but I'll bet it'll be really good." After this last sentence, both Dad and I allowed for a pause in order to be certain that she had concluded her observations. Dad seemed to consider all of this before chiming in with his own contribution, "Yeah, it's really green."

If "God is in the details," then Mom must spend more time with God than all the leaders of the world's religions combined. Whenever she visits Erika and me, she inevitably points out at least one aspect of our house or yard that we have never noticed before, though we have lived there for nearly twenty years. Growing up, she was the only one in our family who would fix things that had broken, and usually did so by staring at the broken item, considering what materials she had access to, and then coming up with a repair plan that can only be described as MacGyver-esque. Our childhood home was filled with projects in various stages of completion that would occupy much of her free time (and, to her children's annoyance, much of the house's free space). She's also the kind of person who gets up early and has a hard time sitting still until she heads to bed in the early evening—a natural-born "putterer."

Dad has many of the opposite characteristics. It's not that he's unobservant, per se. It's just that he's always been more concerned with the big picture. To be sure, if you engage with him about world history or how best to utilize a staff of relief pitchers, he can recall details and speak to circumstances that are incredibly specific. But if you discuss theology or philosophy, the conversation can be much more esoteric, getting to the nature of human beings and our desire to connect to a higher power. When we talk, it's often more about *how* we're doing rather than *what* we're doing. Unlike Mom, he's always been able to sit for long periods of time, content to explore his own thoughts, preferring not to be distracted by activities designed only to keep us busy. Like Bob, his introspection can cause him to miss details of conversations, which he famously brings up long after the topic has shifted.

Although both ways of being have their idiosyncrasies, neither is right or wrong. It's just how my parents are. It would be ridiculous of me to denigrate any of these characteristics, in no small part because I also see them in myself. My natural default is to be more like Dad; I generally view life through a wide lens. Especially when dealing with university students, who can easily get mired in the minutiae of their immediate situations, I often find myself reminding them to also focus on long-term goals and to think beyond the microcosm of college life—just because things are like this here and now doesn't mean they're like this everywhere or will be forever.

This is my natural approach to music, as well. I love to let the sounds wash over me, exploring my immediate, visceral reactions to what I'm hearing. I never get restless or bored listening to full-length Mahler symphonies, many of which take more than an hour to perform. When becoming familiar with operas and musicals, I often prefer listening to audio recordings over seeing fully staged productions because I can focus better on the music, the voices, and the story being told without the additional details of costumes, sets, and lighting (which, though crucial storytelling elements in staged works, can pull my attention from the music).

I have to acknowledge, however, that I am a better musician when I also remember to take Mom's approach and dig in on the details. Instead of just following my emotional reaction to the music, I consider its formal construction and analyze its harmonic content. I look at the way composer/poet (or composer/lyricist) teams set melodies to text, trying to understand the intention behind their choices. I explore various perspectives that could impact the way the material is presented, knowing that there are "many roads to Rome" and that my interpretations may not ring true or feel authentic to an audience or to my students.

Mom's approach also informs my teaching. I do not subscribe to the idea that my students come to me to have their voices "fixed." We can all find ways to build skill, expressivity, and efficiency in our singing, but that doesn't mean that what they are doing when they come to their lessons is "wrong" or "broken." That being said, I do use Mom's fix-it approach by observing, inquiring as to what goals the students are wanting to achieve, coming up with a plan (knowing, again, that there are many possible options to get to a desired result), and working with the materials and information available to me to get those results.

Of course, I am at my best as a teacher when I am also utilizing Dad's approach. Although I am not trained to delve into the scope of practice of a "counselor," as Dad is, I have to observe and be attentive to *how* my students are doing, not just *what* they are doing. In the same way, it doesn't always help my students when I bog them down with the details of respiration, phonation, registration, and resonance. Sometimes, they need to focus instead on emotion, affect, and even the occasional image rather than placing their attention on the biomechanics of singing. I believe that music and the arts, and especially singing, are ultimately about human connection. Though the work of a voice teacher has to include helping students create sounds that are sustainable and as efficiently produced as possible for each individual, the purpose is to communicate text and tones that can create a lasting impact on a listener. So far, the best way I've come up with to get that result is to imitate both Mom and Dad.

Sensory Excitement

In a similar way, because Bob's senses are such a key part of his own learning process and how he experiences the world, he views sensation as a gateway to the intellect. In fact, it seems anathema to him to be able to intellectualize something without having experienced it first through one of the senses. "I guess we could debate what 'intellectual' means in this case," he says, "but I first experience the intellectual through the five senses. I don't know how else you can get information into the body, other than through the eyes, nose, ears, all of the senses. I don't know how else you learn."

Bob recalls moments when both his senses and his intellect were overwhelmed. The first time he visited the Art Institute in Chicago, as an undergraduate, was one of those times. "I couldn't believe my eyes. I thought, how am I going to get through the entirety of this place?" he says. "We were taken there by the art teacher in our basic art history course, Nancy Douglas. Every brushstroke, every carving in a piece of marble just threw her over the edge with excitement, to the point that people thought she was kind of nutty. And, for the very same reason, people probably think I'm kind of nutty."

He had a similar experience at the Museum of Modern Art when he lived in New York City in the 1970s. "At that time, you could get very close to paintings, within inches of them," he says. "When Sandy and I went to see Picasso's *Guernica*, there was a cord around the painting, limiting the distance you could approach to look at it. But we were still within inches, just beyond arm's length. That painting struck my eyes and stirred me emotionally. I learned not to show too much excitement because I didn't want people to look at me as a fool, like I was out of my mind. But I was churning. When I later saw *Guernica* again in 2001 in Madrid's Prado Museum, we were what seemed to be almost a half city block away from it. Your time was limited, there was bulletproof glass in front of the painting, and the guards kept moving you, which didn't allow for the same experience."

He recognizes that some people might interpret these qualities, especially his excitability, as childlike. He embraces that assessment, due in no small part to the fact that he sees many of the same reactions in his young grandson. Perhaps this is an example of the "grand-apple" not falling far from the tree. Or perhaps Bob just never lost the childlike ability to be excited by his senses. "It's interesting to watch my grandson, who is two years old, when he's stimulated by something he hears, sees, tastes, or feels," he says. "In fact, he did it this morning. They were going to go to a place called Monkey Business where children are allowed to jump on trampolines. And so, knowing where he was going, I asked him this morning, 'Liam, where are you going today?' He said, 'Monkey biz-miss!' And he raised his arms and shook his body. I don't know if I did that as a child, but I know I was just as easily stirred."

Throughout his life, the surest way for Bob to feel stirred was through music. "I was always turned on in music because of the feeling," he says. "So, I think initially, music needs to stir you. You've got to allow it, somehow, some way, to stir you. It certainly did stir me, even more so if I had a score and I could follow the notes. Then I could feel the score and see the music. So I had music driving me and provoking me, not only through the ears, but also through the sense of touch and through the sense of sight. It can stir you. It can excite you. If you don't have those senses, how else are you going to deal with music? If you listen to it passively, it must be utterly boring. That's to be pitied. Very, very much pitied."

Sympathetic Vibrations

I think Bob is onto something here related to how humans perceive sound, in particular. I've long believed that singers relate to the world—not just music—through sound. It's often not enough for us simply to hear something. It isn't truly real, or fully experienced, until we can recreate those sounds and feel them in our own bodies. I suspect that's why musical people are constantly singing along with the melodies we hear. And it isn't just songs that we vocalize. I often find myself repeating the lines delivered by news anchors, with the same inflection they use, as I ponder the meaning of what they're saying. I harmonize with the beeps I hear when elevator doors open, trains approach, or when ringing up items at the grocery store self-check. I also receive befuddled looks from my cats when I repeat their meows back to them, even if I have to whistle in order to match their pitch in the correct octave. That may be an annoying habit for onlookers (human or feline), but I know I'm not the only singer who does this.

I think the phrase "That really resonates with me" is significant for singers. We literally feel sounds within us as air molecules are put into motion and pass through the spaces of our vocal tracts, setting tissues into motion, and creating the sensations of forced resonance as the hard surfaces within our bodies sympathetically vibrate. This is how we experience music. It is visceral. It literally moves us inside. We often have difficulty participating passively, as listeners only. Music inspires us as we breathe it in, exciting more than just our eardrums, and frequently initiating a full-body oscillation that makes it difficult to sit still. Perhaps we should more consciously (and more often) revel in that experience.

6 "What Is an Art Song, Anyway?"
Intellectual Enlightenment and Musical Bias

Early in his tenure at the University of Colorado, Bob attended a lecture one of his colleagues gave titled "What's an art song, anyway?" It was a play on the Leonard Bernstein lyric in "My Name is Barbara" from the song cycle *I Hate Music*: "What's a baby-bush, anyway?" He admits to being "absolutely enthralled" with the question of what an art song is, and he continued to ponder it long after the lecture. "That question was always in the forefront of my foolish head," he says. "I had to try to get to the bottom of that, because we're teaching art song—French art song literature, German art song literature—and I don't know what the hell that term means." Is it just an academic term, designed to be snooty? He suspected not, but in the absence of a satisfying definition, he couldn't say for sure.

He spent many years asking graduate students, often in doctoral qualifying exams, "Can you define for me what an art song is?" In some exams, it would be the only question he would put forth. "Oh, the stammering," he recalls. "We've got a lot of terms such as this in our business that we throw around, though few can actually define them. What *is* the difference between an art song and, for instance, a pop song?"

It bears repeating that the power of music to excite the senses was something Bob felt and understood from early in his life. But the more he pursued formal music studies, the more he expected from his musical experiences. It was no longer enough for music to simply stir him physically or emotionally. He wanted something deeper.

After much deliberation, he eventually settled on a definition. "What I figured it came down to was this: An art song is a song in which the components of the song enlighten a listener intellectually. If it comes with a side of entertainment, fine. If it comes with a side of emotion—such as hatred, loss, new love—fine. But what it has to have is a poem that enlightens one's intellect and to be paired with music which is also enlightening, as opposed to just entertaining." By this definition, he is not only describing the work of Franz Schubert, Gerald Finzi, Libby Larson, and the like. He also includes much of the music of Pink Floyd, The Beatles, and Harold Arlen. "Popular music, in my mind, can be art," he says. Neither should this assume that every song written by these composers should automatically be assumed to reside within the art song category. "Not everybody is going to hit a home run every time they swing the bat," he says. "Schubert didn't. You can look through his 610 songs and find some trash."

Bob also believes that art songs offer listeners something personal and significant about its creators. "It reveals the inner thoughts, the neurological behavior, if you will, of a composer—someone who came upon a particular text and was so provoked that he or she had no choice but to put music to it and interpret it through a chosen set of rhythms and pitches," he says. "First of all, they need to pick a damn good poem. And second of all, they have to enlighten that poem and artistically reveal their thoughts of how it can be interpreted through their music."

Naturally, there can be disagreements when individuals make these subjective assessments, which Bob welcomes. "Happily, I've gotten myself into all sorts of troubles and upset some people by saying things like, 'If Richard Strauss hadn't written his operas, I probably would have deemed him a mediocre composer. He was just nothing but a pop song composer.'" He justifies these opinions, saying, "The poetry isn't all that deep and he writes in a musical language that you don't have to be that musically savvy to be moved by." After making these intentionally inflammatory comments and engaging in some lively debate, he would often walk back some of what he said, but not without offering one more opinion. "'OK, maybe he was an art song composer,' I'd say, 'but not to the degree that Schubert was!'"

Of course, before a song can enlighten an audience, it first has to have an intellectual impact on the singer who chooses to perform it. "I find this absolutely important," Bob says, "that we be enlightened ourselves. If we're not enlightened by what's on the page, then we're wasting our time." In his own assessments, when he had been satisfied as to the quality of an art song, it would then make his list of selections that he would draw from when assigning repertoire to students in his studio. As an advocate and teacher of musical art, he felt a responsibility to not simply address the "songs for the folks") need not be intellectually stimulating if their purpose is just to get everyone singing together (something that may be more difficult to accomplish with a Schubert song—depending, of course, on who is gathered).

That being said, there is nothing wrong with identifying criteria for distinguishing between music that is intentionally, intellectually stirring—perhaps by innovating or exploring the boundaries of a genre, or by creating new genres—and music that is designed to have mass appeal. Certainly, I have plenty of both kinds of music in my playlists. As described earlier, before an assessment of quality can take place, two primary questions could be considered: "What is this music attempting to do?" and "How well is it accomplishing those goals?"

Musical Bias

Regardless of genre, and despite his definitions and criteria, Bob does feel that he always gives music an honest chance. Frequently, it is his daughters who introduce him to certain songs or performers. He always appreciates the spirit with which they bring him songs, knowing that they feel moved enough to share them. And many of these songs elicit positive reactions from their music professor father. Other times, however, he is quick to level the opposite opinion. "Sometimes I say, 'Uh-uh, I ain't going to listen to that, because it's dumbing me down,'" he says. "I want to be lifted up, not emotionally, but intellectually." He would not lobby such opinions, however, without providing details or explaining his reasoning (when his daughters would welcome such details). "I think we have that responsibility, as learned musicians, not to be erudite, but to share why we feel an audience should listen to a piece of music."

Part of why Bob intentionally seeks out vocal music from many genres, and considers a great many of them to fall within the art song category, is that he felt many of his colleagues over the years displayed an alarming amount of what he calls "musical bias," even for genres within the Western classical canon. "I don't understand why people are so damn biased," he says. "Telling somebody you sang a Schoenberg piece in college and they respond, 'Oh, why did you have to do that?' Or trying to convince me that music written after 1800 is better music than anything that was written prior to it—that bullshit."

that I must be an artist. But I've always been hesitant to refer to myself in that way. I call myself a singer, since that is my instrument. And I call myself a musician, since that is my medium. Ultimately, however, I think it's up to each audience member to decide if what I do is artistic or not. Certainly, I *aspire* to be an artist, and I approach performances with a process that I hope brings that aspiration into manifestation. But I'm just not comfortable giving that subjective honorific to myself.

To be sure, some believe Enya is an artist and some do not, though it would be difficult to deny her popularity (evidenced by album sales alone). Some likely believe that certain Enya songs and performances are artistic, while others may fall into the category of simply being popular. To each their own. We all get to decide for ourselves based on our own criteria, as Bob does by establishing his own definition of what an art song is to him.

Of course, I have to recognize the privilege and bias that exist in my own musical assessments. Though I have graduate degrees in music, the sort of music the educational system where I earned those degrees traditionally teaches us to value is overwhelmingly (and problematically) white, male-dominated, and Eurocentric. That influence is something I have to acknowledge and sometimes look past when evaluating music that comes from outside those specific categories. In many cases, I don't have sufficient education or background to fully appreciate the intellectually enlightening capacities of music from cultures outside my own or those that were not part of my formal education. When this is true, the only lens through which I can assess the music may be how it entertains or emotionally engages me. Once again, allowing that people can have a variety of experiences with, and reactions to, music, I hesitate to assume that anyone's experiences are lesser than mine simply because we may have different criteria for the purpose we expect music to serve.

It's also important to mention that sometimes the primary purpose of a piece of music might simply be to give the people engaging with it something to do together. Channeling the work of author Christopher Small,[1] and following up on the premise that music is ultimately about connection (humans connecting with each other, connecting to something greater than themselves, connecting to their cultures, connecting to thoughts/ideas/poems/songs—some of which have existed for generations), the degree to which a song encourages full-throated participation may be the primary component by which its effectiveness is measured—how *can* I keep from singing? Folk songs (literally

If a song seems not to be particularly intellectually stirring, we can try to discover what the music *is* designed to do and can then evaluate how successful it is at accomplishing its intended goal. For instance, music used in commercials is designed to increase the desirability of the goods or products being sold (or to inspire emotional states in potential consumers that make them more likely to spend their money). I can acknowledge, assess, and even appreciate how well music in these situations accomplishes those outcomes (and, perhaps, this process will also help me avoid any subconscious influencing the companies hope to wield). Music that underscores dialogue in movies is intended to help convey the emotions the characters are experiencing on screen. Music used in high-impact workout videos is designed to facilitate aerobic activity and increase heart rates. The same music in each of these examples may feel unsatisfying when removed from these contexts and placed in a concert hall. But, if they were not intended to be used in the concert hall, it would be misguided to apply the rubric of "art music" in their assessment. When we get to the "why," we can recognize the role a piece of music is playing, and can both assess and enjoy it for that, without expecting it to be something it is not meant to be.

Personally, I have no particular love or disdain for Enya's "Sail Away." It doesn't thrill me, but it doesn't cause me to grit my teeth, either (orthodontic associations aside). I do, however, find Enya's version of "How Can I Keep from Singing?" to be quite profound. Of course, neither the text nor the melody was created by Enya. Still, I find its lyrics to be tremendously thought-provoking (In Bob's language, "She picked a damn good poem."). The problem I find with the piece when it is sung as a hymn, as I have heard in many churches of various denominations, is that if the tempo is too fast, the depth of the lyrics can be glossed over. By simply altering the rhythm and spacing out the phrases, as Enya does, listeners are encouraged to hear each thought individually as well as in the context of the entire poem. In a similar way, the sustained nature of the synthesized instrumentation allows the sounds to echo and linger, reflecting the way the thoughts are suspended in my mind at the end of each phrase. In this way, words and music work together to invoke a spirit of meditation and thoughtfulness that enlightens the mind and, yes, entertains, as well.

Does that make Enya an artist? Who's to say? "Artist" might be just as difficult a term to define as "art song" and is probably just as subjective. For instance, people may assume, because I have been educated and trained in music, technical elements of the songs he assigned. Rather, he was obligated to help students understand why he felt they qualified as art songs. He often did this through detailed explorations of the many sonorities found within a song in order to discover how those sounds aid (or hinder) the expression of the text. This approach helped students develop their own creative artistry by moving beyond passive listening and delving into "why" a piece of music may strike us. "As a teacher, I have that responsibility," he says. "We all have that responsibility, to draw students' ears to what is musically important, textually important."

In contrast to art songs, Bob feels that popular music is focused primarily on making listeners feel an emotion. "If something is built just to make you feel good, to the point where you will go out and buy my recording, buy my sheet music, download my sheet music, but it doesn't enlighten me, I declare that as. popular," he says. He points out how a primary goal of pop music is for it to be sold to the masses (the general "pop"-ulation) in order to generate income. Therefore, the lyrics and musical organization must be immediately understandable so as to be consumable by a wide-ranging audience. Bob feels songs written in this way risk becoming vehicles for emotional manipulation. "Why were all of these buildings and concert halls built at this university if we're just giving performances that make people feel good, sad, indifferent, or whatever else?" he says. "Great art should enlighten."

He feels a key example of a pop song, by his definition, is "Sail Away" by Enya. "I used to hear that damn thing at 6:30 in the morning at our daughter's orthodontist appointments for years and years," he says. "I can't think of any song that is more shallow. But it's popular!"

How Can I Keep from Singing?

Some of what Bob says here gives me pause. In my experience, I find that when we probe the "why" of a piece of music, we are better equipped to assess its value. This applies to all music, not just art music. For this reason, if people are drawn to pop music (or any other genre) simply because it makes them feel good, I honor that as a perfectly valid response to a musical stimulus, especially if the music was written specifically to evoke an emotion. I don't believe that every composition has to necessarily bear the responsibility of striking an audience's intellect in order to have value.

In most cases, he views this as simple ignorance. "If someone says to me, 'I just can't listen to the music of Webern,' I'll ask, 'Oh, which Webern pieces have you listened to? What pieces do you hate?' You have to know something about Webern to make such an assessment," he says. "I could buy your qualitative judgment if you'd listen to the music. But if you haven't eaten the steak, you can't criticize the quality of the beef."

He does recognize inherent bias in the field of Western classical music, namely the unmistakable preference given to a select group of composers. "No one would have been caught teaching Russian music when I was in school, or the music of any Eastern Bloc country, because of the Cold War. We did not learn Spanish music or Latin American music. Those were not taught," he says. Women composers, when mentioned at all, were either relegated to the periphery or discussed in relation to a male composer who was more prominently remembered. "It was only the European white male who seemed to matter," he says. He regrets these gaps in his own formal education and wonders at the richness left behind by these omissions.

Nonetheless, he is grateful that he was taught to assess music on an individual basis rather than to discard it simply because it was composed outside of the favored eras or genres. He can readily point to colleagues who would never consider assigning music to their students from, for instance, the Medieval or Renaissance eras. "I didn't have any such fences put around me by any one of my teachers. That I remember," he says. "That was probably the main reason I was hired at IU. I was even told so—that I came in without musical biases."

At CU, Bob taught the German and French song literature courses. In that capacity, he felt strongly that he should provide students with the full breadth of vocal music history. Oftentimes, he felt that early music was given short shrift, both in these courses and in the repertoire that many of his colleagues assigned in the voice studio.

Bob feels there is much to be gained from performing the songs (not just the arias) of Haydn, Mozart, and Beethoven—even for students on the "opera performance" track. He finds tremendous value in exploring the vocal works of Dowland and Purcell, a pursuit that goes beyond any technical gains those works may bring to vocal studies. "Some teachers would assign works written prior to the 19th century just as a way to warm up the voice," Bob says. "It was just 'a cocktail and a canape' before the 'real music' could begin. Are you kidding me? That was the conventional wisdom at the time."

He appreciates the advice he was once given that, even though his voice was not the appropriate *fach* to perform the music of Verdi and Wagner on stage, he should still sing it. "You should sing some of that music so that you know what those notes feel like in your throat," Bob says. "That builds another tier of information that you can share with a student when you teach a Verdi or Wagner aria. Just because I'm not going to perform Wagner doesn't mean I should not know anything about Wagner."

The same philosophy extends to those who *will* perform Verdi and Wagner—he feels they should be encouraged to sing early music as a way to know the music, composers, and style of that period of Western classical history. "That doesn't mean I'm going to subject an audience to 150 verses of Hildegard von Bingen," he says. "But I did ask students to sing her music."

Bob does feel that he was able to win over some of his colleagues on this point. "What they could eventually see is that, in graduate oral exams, the students came in with better preparation when they had performed a wide variety of music. When they were up against questions from the academics, the historians, and the theorists, they could talk about that at some level and refer to it. If nothing else, hopefully it did to them what those faculty-led listening events did for me when I was an undergraduate. They raised curiosity. That's what I always had—curiosity. And I think that's what got me as far as I was able to get in this business."

Bob credits Bettina Bjorksten, yet again, as an influence and an example in this realm. "I ended up learning something from her that I wasn't prepared for, that I didn't anticipate," he says. "What she taught me was the importance of being an unbiased musician." He recounts when Bjorksten told him about taking her granddaughter to a rock concert. Afterward, she said to him, "Robert, it was one of the finest musical experiences of my life. The intellectual level at which they were playing and performing just overwhelmed me." As he says when recalling this memory, "That was unexpected."

Bob again notes the inclination to allow his ears to focus his attention as another reason for his lack of musical bias. Once stirred, the intellectual explorations begin. "Give me some sound and I get excited," he says. "That does not mean that there could be some other reasons to dislike the piece, on an intellectual plane. But, nonetheless, I was always attracted to sound."

It was through Bob's studies of music theory that he was able to bridge his sensory-driven experience of music to a deeper, intellectual understanding.

Though the sounds of music could always draw him in, he wanted to have the theoretical skills to make informed, qualitative judgments about what he was hearing. Though these studies were not easy for him, and he always noticed that it took him longer to complete assignments than it did many of his peers, he was determined to make the grade. "In my master's degree, my goal was, 'I'm going to get this.' And I did," he says.

This knowledge allowed him to identify structure and form in music. "I then realized, if a song shows decent organization—because music has its own kind of architecture—if it has form, I can start to see that song's design." He began to make connections between musical structure and the structure of buildings. "A building can be designed very well, but if the engineering, the organization, or the structure is lacking, it's not a good building," he says.

As his musical intellect developed and he formed the ability to listen at a deeper level, he was provoked to listen to as much music as he could. "Prior to that," he says, "I was listening to music, and liked it just based on how it made me feel, which is pretty self-absorbing. I admit, I was turned on in music because of the feeling. Initially, music needs to stir you. And you've got to allow it to stir you. But to have the ability to talk about a piece of music on an intellectual level stimulated my heart and my mind."

As he reflects on these thoughts, he makes a concession. "Yes, the intellectual stimulation still made me feel good. I guess, on some level, even that can be seen as self-serving. But I never thought of it that way. I always thought that if I could talk intellectually about a piece of music and add that tier to it, I'm actually serving music at a better level, with more respect. And music can't serve itself. It comes out of a human mind, and it must be taught through a human mind."

Performance as Service

This discussion acknowledges an age-old question: As musicians, is our primary responsibility to serve music, to serve the creators of that music, or to serve each other through music? Bob almost contradicts himself a bit on this point. Though he states his desire to serve music, he also admits a responsibility to honor the individuals who created that music. He also acknowledges that his desire to serve music caused him at times to lose his patience with musicians, especially if he perceived them to be placing themselves at the center of this hierarchy. Does this mean he places music above musicians (the art above the people engaged in the art)? I believe it is quite the contrary. Rather, in his mind, when we are in service to music, we are in service to each other. The greater our devotion to the art, the greater we serve composers, artists, and audiences alike, which is why he adheres so strictly to his principles.

"We must not lose sight, nor must I lose sight, either, of the purpose of music," Bob says. "It's not just to write something to put onto a shelf of a library. It is a language. And I think we have a responsibility to our fellow human beings to never lie to them when we are communicating through music and words. Part of humility means being truthful. In order to be truthful with music, we have to study it to the highest level. I would often say, 'I'm giving you what I deem, today, to be the truth. If I don't know something and can't answer your questions, I will go and study to see if I can get an answer. You do the same; we'll come back and compare notes.'"

Therefore, he reveals himself—perhaps despite himself—when he admits that honoring the details of music not only honors the composers but is the surest path to stimulate audiences in a way that serves our fellow humans. If the point of a performance is to give audience members a personal, transformative experience, the performer, then, becomes the vessel through which the composer's and poet's ideas are brought—through the language of music—to a listener. As performers, we serve as the vessels of this transference, but we are not empty vessels. We get to have a personal influence on how the material is delivered. Performers, then, must have sufficient humility to allow ideas to pass through them without distorting their original intent while also being confident enough to believe they can personalize the material in a way that brings new or unique meaning to listeners. This can only be done if the performers believe both the music and their own performance of it deserve to be heard. That can easily allow performances to morph into ego trips if the emphasis swings too much toward the "self" of the performer at the expense of accurately relaying the intent of the original creators. Therefore, the balance between a performer's confidence and humility, though perhaps delicate to strike, is crucial to authentic performance.

"We have a responsibility to deliver the truth as we know it," Bob says. "You want students to understand that and act similarly. Like [former IU cello professor] János Starker would say to students, 'My job is to upset you.' If I'm going to upset you, as a teacher, it's going to be with the truth, as I understand it, each and every day. Because you've got to perform with integrity, with truth."

Reflecting on these ideas, Bob recognizes that there are many elements of this field, beyond the music itself, that can be humbling and awe-inspiring when we stop to acknowledge them. "Recognizing the amount of money that is being paid by students and/or their parents, I owe them something profound in exchange. Recognizing, too, the investment of the state of Indiana and donors to erect, build, and develop a music school—that's a great expense. Add to that the shelves of manuscripts in the library, which are records of intimate thoughts—it isn't just their intellectual property, it's intimate material, which deserves to be protected and honored. Therefore, we have a responsibility to get on the stage or in the classroom and communicate, with honesty, at the highest level. You know when you have been ripped off just as much as I do. And that's why I'm not all that well liked, in many circles, because I call people on it. There are charlatans, but I can't be so cynical as to think that the world is made up of them. I do believe that I'm around more good people than I am bad. I still have hope that we are around good people in this field who understand what we owe the student and the listener."

These firmly held beliefs are what finally led to his retirement from teaching. After more than twenty years at the University of Colorado and an additional ten years at Indiana University, he decided it was time to step down at the age of sixty-five. "I knew that I would be shortchanging the students on the truth," he says. "It's not that I would ever lie or deceive. But I knew that I was incapable of working as hard as I used to in order to deliver the truth. When I realized that, that's when I retired."

Note

1 Christopher Small, *Musicking: The Meanings of Performing and Listening* (Middletown, CT: Wesleyan University Press, 1998).

7 Selfless Communication
Teaching Artistry

As can be surmised from what has been presented thus far, the ultimate goal of Bob's teaching—the overriding purpose of his studio voice lessons—was not to develop efficiently produced sounds or even to help singers create beautiful tones, although much of singing voice training tends to focus heavily on these two elements. While singers and teachers often obsess about fashioning beautifully resonant sonorities, one of the ironies of these efforts is that audiences will often accept imperfect singing—and less polished voices—if songs are performed with great communicative intent and delivery. "The goal of all of this," Bob says, "is to communicate at a level where you literally can change your listener in the time during which you perform."

Although this is a great responsibility, no singer (or singer/pianist duo) is left alone in the process. "You are delivering a recitation of text and music, rhythm and pitch, which are under the control of a composer and poet. And what they put on the page is very telling as to their inner thoughts," he says. "We have an actual record of some individuals' thinking. Meaning, what you see in a page of music is what once coursed through someone's mind. We have a view into that and we have a responsibility to deliver that to our listeners to the best of our abilities."

Bob believes that responsibility should be at the fore during voice lessons—not just building well-tuned "singing machines" but promoting expressive artistry. "Why do we do all of this? I must say, I think we've lost a bit of that today in our teaching, if I were to be frank," he says. "Why are we doing these exercises? Why are we so careful about getting breath into us and breath out of us? Well, because we've got quite an altarpiece here to share. If you don't like a piece of music, don't perform it. But if you're going to pick up a book of songs that once coursed through the minds of a poet and a composer, you have a real responsibility to take this seriously, and to build the finest technique possible that allows you to communicate this song—selflessly. That was very much a part of my teaching. I insisted upon that. There were times when I was probably deemed to be uncompromising about that, and rightly so. No, there was no other way."

According to Bob, this commitment to communication should exist regardless of the performance venue. Whether singing on stage at the Metropolitan Opera, in a student recital, or even in more casual gatherings, the goal is the same. "My father would sometimes ask me to sing something for him or for family members," he recalls. "He'd say, 'Bob, will you sing for us? Sing something like "Jesus Loves Me."' No matter where you are, you bear the responsibility to communicate fully and passionately and change someone's life by your performance. That's so overlooked."

Bob's preference for artistry over vocal quality was not limited to singers of the Western classical realm. Along with Schwarzkopf, he adds Barbra Streisand to the short list of singers whom he regards as the finest of the last 100 years. "Bar none," he says, "because of their communication skills and their abilities to go to the most uncomfortable places of thinking, the most dangerous places of thinking, where they find freedom."

Though we are now well into the twenty-first century, Bob does not believe that the brand of artistry exemplified by the likes of Schwarzkopf and Streisand is outdated or an old-fashioned relic of the past. In fact, he believes that audiences today have just as great a desire for artistic connection as they ever have. This brand of communication, he believes, surpasses musical genre, formal music training, and even generation. "I think I am as willing to be engaged as I ever was. Even more so, actually, as I realize I'm in the winter of my life," he says. "I still have room for someone to really engage me and to really turn me on to a message through music that I've not heard before. And I wait for that to happen. There's a lot of room in the arts for greatness—for somebody to set us on fire, as [Maria] Callas did."

Bob admits that his willingness—indeed, desire—to be meaningfully impacted by music does not always manifest itself in positive ways. He instilled the responsibility to "change the listener" into his students and he expects no less when he is the one listening. "As my wife says from time to time, 'Bob, you can be a cynic, and you are most of the time.' And it's true," he says. "But I like to think that my cynicism is due to the stimulus of foolishness. And it deserves cynicism at its best."

Practically speaking, he believes the pendulum has swung so far in the direction of prioritizing beautiful sounds that it results in a lack of communication. Even the most lovely voice can start to sound banal in a performance if there is not a deep commitment to communication (and a story worth communicating). Bob identifies what he feels is the root of the problem. "What I believe has happened is that singers are not being guided to say something special and unique. They color within the lines," he says. "As a result, we have this boring level of performance where everybody just kind of sounds the same."

He points out how, in the 1960s, a full one-third of the Arts & Leisure section of *The New York Times* was filled with performance announcements: choral concerts, solo recitals, operas, and other performances. "And now?" he asks. "You're lucky if they fit on half of a page." He recalls the days of sold-out halls for song recitals by the likes of Schwarzkopf, Dietrich Fischer-Dieskau, and Elly Ameling. "And why? Because there was something very engaging going on. These people spoke to an audience."

Early in his retirement, he attended occasional performances, but most left him feeling unsatisfied. Still today, friends, colleagues, and family members recommend performers to him whom he can watch online. But he has yet to find someone he feels is saying something truly unique. "The cynic in me says that everybody's kind of the same," he says. "I can't listen to it. It's just dullsville. Just nothing going on. People moan and groan and say that you couldn't be a recitalist today. It's just not profitable. Wanna bet? You could make a lot of money as a recitalist if you had something special and unique to say. There's a lot of room out there for communicative singing, and a lot of money to be made."

Generational Trends

Respectfully, I do not share Bob's cynicism, although I believe I understand its roots. Part of the reason I can't go along with it is that I can't afford to. My job depends on my ability to foster development of both skills and creativity. If singers come to voice lessons with less-developed capacities for communicative singing, it is my responsibility to help them build those capabilities. I know Bob believes this, too. In fact, I think his primary frustration is that he doesn't feel teachers today are spending enough time on artistry and communication skills, perhaps believing they are simply inherent rather than developed. More on that later. Regardless, identifying the problem is the first step to addressing it, which makes me hopeful that I can be an active part of the solution rather than cynical that it is something that will never change.

Another reason I have trouble accepting Bob's cynicism is that I generally have a strong negative reaction to any opinions that hint at how everyone was better off in the "good ol' days." I have equal impatience for the exasperated exhortations of, "these kids today" especially when coming from people whose daily exposure to "these kids" is generally low—or who raised the children who are now raising "these kids." Certainly, though we are all individuals, there are generational trends that influence arts, culture, politics, and the like. To be sure, not all of the trends embraced by the current younger generations enthuse me. Indeed, as Bob expresses above, some of these trends cause me great concern (I suppose there is a bit of curmudgeon within me after all). But I try not to immediately label these trends as better or worse—they are simply different. And I try to be purposeful in not immediately labeling what is different as "less than." It takes time to fairly evaluate any generation's overall impact on society, and I suspect that it can only be done in hindsight, which none of us have the benefit of at this moment. Undoubtedly, some of today's contributions will be remembered positively and some negatively.

As an example, in the 1990s and early 2000s, journalist Tom Brokaw became a *New York Times* best-selling author with books hailing those who lived through the Great Depression and fought in the Second World War as "the greatest generation." No doubt, there is much to celebrate and honor in those who lived through this era and fought against the destructive forces of the time. However, no generation got everything right or has a monopoly on greatness. The people of this era that Brokaw lauds so enthusiastically also collectively failed horribly when it came to overcoming and eliminating racial discrimination (redlining, segregation, etc.) and advancing equal rights for women and for the LGBTQIA+ community. Those good ol' days were not so good for everyone.

I have witnessed what I would perceive to be positive characteristics as well as negative characteristics in people of all ages. Therefore, I cannot subscribe to wholesale generational assessments. Notions that Bob has articulated, like "Singers [today] are not being guided to say something special and unique," could be true in some instances while not holding up in others. Accounting for the role of subjectivity in the arts, it is also likely that aficionados on all sides can make convincing (and vehement) arguments about what they believe constitutes expressive artistry and who is and isn't performing with it.

At the same time, I have also noticed in more recent generations an increasing fear of being "wrong." Especially when it comes to singing, a fixed mindset often prevails with many students who believe that, unless they have a certain baseline of "talent," they should not pursue singing—even avocationally. There have always been elements of culture that have discouraged singing, from the unnecessarily gendered ("Boys shouldn't sing, it's too feminine.") to mean-spirited offhanded comments ("Wow, you're really tone deaf!") to the self-deprecating ("I couldn't carry a tune in a bucket!"). Indeed, when the reality TV show *American Idol* premiered in 2002, a significant component of how they marketed the show was as an opportunity to collectively mock the singers who lacked professional-level abilities. The show flies in the face of the educational model that singing skills are developed over time with quality instruction and diligent practice. Instead, it implies that "talent" need only be discovered in individuals who can then be plucked from obscurity and thrust, fully polished, into stardom. I am grateful that the teachers I had throughout the years did not subscribe to this mentality, especially when my "talents" were not easily identifiable and clearly needed cultivation.

That being said, and at the risk of generalizing in the same way that I was just criticizing, there is often a tendency found in people of my generation (Gen X) to ignore the voices of earlier generations. Believing that everything has changed too much for older peoples' perspectives to be pertinent or relatable, we relegate them to historical or emeritus status while we get on with the work of today. In my view, this is just as problematic as criticizing the up-and-coming generation for any generalized attributes we might assign them.

Therefore, when someone like Bob, with his years in the industry, expresses perspectives based on his experience, I believe folks like me would do well to listen and try to understand how his perspectives were formed and how they might influence my own work going forward. Bob would be the first one to encourage me to disagree with him or challenge him, and he would happily engage in a spirited discussion of disagreement. Instead of dismissing an opinion like "Singers [today] are not being guided to say something special and unique," I might be better served by examining how it is that singers collectively seem to be performing today in a way that is different from how singers performed a generation or two earlier. Certain elements are easily identifiable. For instance, modern operatic performance venues are generally larger than they used to be, creating a need to sing "bigger" than when performing in smaller halls, which could certainly influence expressivity. (One of my IU professors, who had a long operatic career, once said to me, "Part of what makes opera so difficult is that you have to sing almost as loud as you can for almost the entire time.") Contemporary performances of Golden Age musical theater productions indicate that tone quality is trending toward brighter sounds, rather than warmer, changing the palette of expressive colors from which singers may choose. Also, recording technology has developed substantially, such that professional recordings can be mixed, tweaked, and aurally "airbrushed" in a way that should cause us all to question how much any recorded performance may compare to hearing unamplified, live performances. I suppose factors like these could lead singers to prioritize creating certain qualities of sound over other elements of performance, like expressivity.

I remember the point in my training when I made an intentional shift away from always trying to make a big and beautiful sound to instead looking for the vocal sonority that best expressed the message I was intending to communicate. Given this perspective, the only sounds I would classify as "wrong" were the ones that were not delivered with communicative intent. If my experience is generalizable, the shift to prioritizing the most expressive sound instead of the most beautiful sound may take longer for singers training in classical and operatic genres, where beauty of tone holds a prominent place. A greater degree of latitude often exists in musical theater, since primacy is given to the communication of text and stories. Theater artists know they are allowed to make a range of sounds during performances, and sometimes the sound that best expresses the intention behind the text may not be particularly beautiful. In opera, however, the expression comes, in part, through the consistent beauty of the tone produced. For example, opera singers rarely, if ever, use breathy tones, growls, screams, or intentionally gritty or rough qualities.

In the end, understanding the potential causes of generational trends and the kind of singing each generation is inherently taught to value may better help me address the beauty of tone versus expressivity issue with students and clients. As noted earlier, however, even though I may agree with some of Bob's assessments, I simply can't afford to bring cynicism into the studio.

Developing Artistry

The pertinent question that has to be addressed is, "Can artistry actually be taught?" Bob's feelings on the topic are quite clear. "If artistry can't be taught, then I've done nothing with my career and you're doing nothing with yours," he says. "Don't give me that old rubbish!" Even so, there are many (teachers, students, and audience members) who believe such skills are simply inherent—that some artists possess a natural "it factor" that makes them compelling on stage or allows them to communicate more successfully through music than other artists. Although there is certainly a wide range of natural abilities or inclinations that individuals bring to their singing, Bob disagrees with the overall premise that singers are either born with artistry or they aren't. "I always got so riled up when colleagues would congratulate me on the performance of a student and say, 'You know, Bob, that kind of musical expression just can't be taught. They're born with it.' Bullshit!" he says. "Put that in the book."

Even knowing that such comments were probably meant as compliments to the singers, he still found them insulting. If singing teachers are not helping students develop creative artistry, their job duties essentially boil down to those of technicians. Important as technical work is, building technique is not an end in and of itself. "What I was taught, and spent my time doing," Bob says, "was to take all this technical stuff and use it for the highest purpose—communicating words and music. I think it's lazy of us to say, 'Well, we'll never have another Streisand,' or 'We'll never have another Maria Callas.' Oh no, they're out there. And we, as teachers, have the responsibility to teach our students in a way that gets them as close as they can to that place."

A significant influence in Bob's career, who reinforced many of his beliefs about expressive singing, was British pianist Martin Isepp (1930–2011). His musical career had many notable highlights: serving as an associate conductor of the Metropolitan Opera, conducting for the touring company of the Glyndebourne Festival Opera, and serving as head of music at the Opera Akademie of the Royal Danish Opera in Copenhagen, to name a few. As a collaborative pianist, Isepp performed with many well-known singers of his era, including Hans Hotter, Elisabeth Schwarzkopf, John Shirley-Quirk, Frederica von Stade, and Janet Baker, who was a voice student of Isepp's mother, Hélène. In Bob's view, Isepp was the greatest collaborative pianist since his fellow countryman Gerald Moore (1899–1987)—an educated opinion he formed after extensive observations of Isepp.

The faculty and administration of the University of Colorado College of Music brought Isepp to campus for annual two-week residencies over a period of more than twenty years. Each year, during Isepp's residency, voice lessons and music classes were canceled so that everyone in the community could attend his lectures, workshops, and performances, allowing Bob ample opportunity to absorb his wisdom. Bob was not the only faculty member who made an effort to attend as many of Isepp's presentations as possible. He distinctly remembers famed voice teacher and author Barbara Doscher also attending regularly and taking copious notes.

One of the primary lessons Isepp often repeated, entrenching it in Bob's mind, was the idea that singers and pianists are always at the service of a poet and a composer. "He was adamant about that," Bob says. "If he sensed one iota of students performing in a self-serving way, he would put an end to that. That's from where he came."

In addition to the formal classes, Bob also interacted with Isepp at faculty dinners each year at the end of his residency. These gatherings were always hosted at a faculty member's house, usually that of the chair of the voice area, a position Bob held for ten years. This allowed for the opportunity to speak in a more casual setting and to hear some of Isepp's many stories of working with singers of the highest level and collaborating to create the most expressive performances possible.

One of the approaches Bob used with students to develop artistry was stressing the importance of following the rhythm of the text. Like many teachers, he advocates for accuracy of pitch and rhythm. However, the rhythm he wants to hear is driven more by the poet than the composer—yet another belief he attributes to Schwarzkopf. "Precision of rhythm—verbal rhythm—was something I learned from her," he says. "I could hear it in her singing and in listening to her recordings. The rhythms that she gave were not always Schubert's, though. They were word rhythms."

Following the rhythms of the words means honoring both vowels and consonants. Since the vowels are primarily what convey vocal tone, there is an understandable emphasis in studio instruction on creating vowels that are as resonant as possible. But consonants are also necessary for communicating text, and Bob refused to ignore their importance. "Words are a combination of vowels and consonants," he says. "With me, you may not only use vowels to communicate. At times, I would actually like to have a priority on consonants."

He highlights how consonants have duration, just as vowels do. Voiced consonants—like [v], [z], and nasals ([m], [n], and [ŋ])—have pitch and can be sustained, just like vowels. Unvoiced continuant consonants, like [f], [s], and [ʃ], do not have pitch, but they can be sustained and given duration for expressive purposes. "The composer's giving you the whole word," Bob says. "Why would we want to use just our vocal folds when we could also use unvoiced consonants? We still get paid, even when we aren't uttering a voiced pitch. Active singing is not just vocalizing. It can also include silence and unvoiced sounds."

Bob also believes that stopped or plosive consonants, like [t], [k], and [p], can be given duration by employing an aspirate, unvoiced follow-through. In this way, when giving consonants length, singers can use them to support, rather than inhibit, legato. "We're told that a [t] is a stopped consonant," Bob says. "Well, Jessye Norman taught me otherwise years ago through her singing."

He avoids the frequently used direction of calling for "crisp" consonants when singing. He recognizes the usefulness of this approach in certain situations, like in choral settings when onsets and releases must be coordinated as an ensemble. But that practice need not extend to solo singing, which allows for a different aesthetic. As he analogizes, "I don't like crisp cookies. I actually like my cookies a little soft. I'm just saying that there is more than one way to deliver, for example, the letter 'T'. In my voice studio, singers were always free to give length to consonants if it helped them communicate what they wanted to say."

This is a particularly useful expressive tool in songs set to slower tempos that allow for greater duration of all the sounds contained within a word. "That's one of the great gifts of a slow tempo," Bob says. "The slower the tempo, the longer the duration of consonants as well as vowel sounds. It gives you time to use vocal colors, and to allow those colors to unfold in a way that they can't in, for instance, a Rossini aria. And that's where singing becomes interesting."

These are some of the traits that can help singers enliven text and more effectively reach audiences. "I think the world is just waiting for someone to come alive and change us as listeners," Bob says. "Otherwise, we all taste like the same bottle of milk—homogenized!"

Bob recalls Isepp often saying, "We now have to lift the words and music off the page," which is all the easier to do when a piece has been written by an "enlightening" composer. The memories of Isepp's influence lead to the repetition of a well-worn slogan in the Harrison Studio to be explored in the next chapter: "No Parking."

8 Respiration
No Air, No Sound

Once visitors to the Harrison "studio of glass and class" had taken in all the colorful, shiny objects placed throughout the room, one of the next distinguishing features they were likely to notice was the "No Parking" sign affixed to the side of Bob's grand piano. The reason for the sign is rooted in an interaction he had with a summer voice student he taught at CU. This singer was working in a lesson on a section of a song that had several repeated pitches in a row. After she sang through the phrase, Bob interjected, "I said, 'What's going on here that I don't like is that all of these repeated notes feel like complete carbon copies of the first note.'" He reminded the student that music is rhythmically driven and occurs across time. In fact, when reading music, he believes it would be more accurate if the time signature appeared before the clef since all the successive measures indicate the passing of time—and time changes us. "There is not a single one of us on the face of this earth who is the same after four beats of a measure as we were at the beginning of it," he says. "This is all a part of interpretation, dealing with the combination of text and music."

He drew the student's attention to the music. "I said, 'The rhythms are all four quarter notes in that opening bar, but look how those harmonies underscore the rhythms. You've got four equal quarters, but you don't have four equal harmonies. Look at how the text has been laid on those particular beats. You seemed to be the same person at beat four that you were at beat one. You were unaffected by the second or third quarter note of that string of four quarter notes. That's inexpressive. Use your imagination!'"

The student thought about this for a while and then responded, "So, you're saying I was parking?" When Bob agreed with her assessment, she said, "I need to get you a 'No Parking' sign!" One trip to the hardware store and the sign was placed on the side of the piano as a reminder to all students (Figure 8.1). "Had I not had access to those many weeks of Isepp's teaching," Bob says, "I might still be at the place of enjoying singing that does not heed the idea of 'No Parking.'"

Figure 8.1 Bob wears the Harrison Studio "No Parking" sign. Also visible are some of the mid-century modern art glass vases that adorned the room.

There was another famous sign in the Harrison Studio that reflected another frequently iterated teaching philosophy, this one taped to the front of his door. Often, the first chapter of vocal pedagogy texts is dedicated to respiration. Considered fundamental to the process of singing, it was often one of the first elements of technique Bob addressed in voice lessons. The reason, in his explanation, comes from a simple philosophy: "No air, no sound." The sign on his door that greeted students and visitors alike was a slightly coded version of this philosophy: "No A, no S."

After promoting the slogan for a bit, Bob eventually found that it needed an addendum: "No air, no sound, no dollars." The obvious implication was that inefficient breathing could lead to ineffective singing, which would lead to a lack of employment opportunities as a singer. This necessitated another change to the sign, the final version of which featured the letter A followed by the letter S, followed by a dollar sign with slashes through each of them. Although it may have confused passersby who were unable to decipher its meaning, it had an added air of mischief since, at first glance, it seemed to spell out a word: AS$. The studio of class, indeed.

Respiration Revisited

Breathing has become somewhat of a controversial topic in modern pedagogical circles. Traditionally, there has been much emphasis placed on breathing as a crucial—if not the most crucial—element of vocal technique. Understandably so. After all, no air, no sound, no dollars. Historical voice pedagogue Giovanni Battista Lamperti (1839–1910) stated, "The foundation of all vocal study lies in the control of the breath."[1] Many current singers would agree. For instance, operatic baritone George Gagnidze has stated: "For me, the most important thing for a singer is to know how to breathe correctly. It's the basis for everything. . . . If a singer doesn't know how to breathe, they can't sing in a correct and healthy way. In my opinion, breathing is 70% or 80% of everything."[2]

In recent years, however, many pedagogues have started to posit that we may be placing too much emphasis on breathing during singing training and that it may not be the cure-all for every vocal inefficiency that it has long been advertised to be—perhaps especially so when singing outside of Western classical genres. Part of the argument is that we all breathe every minute of every day in order to simply stay alive. Since it can be assumed that all readers of this book are, in fact, alive, we are probably all pretty accomplished at breathing already.

Of course, breathing to sustain self-amplified, *fortissimo* tones calls for different strategies than breathing to sustain life. Therefore, it's logical to assume that breathing for singing will require greater activity of the respiratory system. That being said, the notion of a universal "singer's breath"—one that focuses on full inhalation accompanied by low abdominal expansion that should be utilized whenever preparing to sing—is being reconsidered in favor of the idea of breathing for a given task.

The first and perhaps most obvious example of when a low, full inhalation may not be necessary is when singing shorter phrases of music. To sing a long, soaring, lyric line of *verismo* opera, a substantial amount of air is necessary. But singing a short phrase of one or two measures (or one or two notes) may not require much of an inhalation at all.

Second, taking what feels to be a full-capacity breath may be counterproductive when singing in genres that require "belting." As author and pedagogue Elizabeth Ann Benson states, "support needs are often minimal" when singing in contemporary commercial music (CCM) styles.[3] As she describes, "Belting is a low-breath flow and high-breath pressure activity," one result of which is that the "money notes" don't use as much air as those in classical-style singing.[4] Therefore, when belting, taking in large amounts of air during inhalation may be unnecessary.

As speech-language pathologist Leda Scearce notes, a substantial inhalation before belting may even be harmful. As she describes, the subglottic pressure necessary for belting is best achieved through vocal fold adduction rather than with abdominal pressure.[5] Therefore, the inhalation posture may be more static than what is used during classical singing. As Scearce warns, an overemphasis on "support" resulting in excessive abdominal tension "can exacerbate traumatic injuries by creating excessive subglottic pressure and increasing mechanical stress on the vocal folds."[6]

Voice scientist Johan Sundberg found that a "belly out" inhalation strategy, accompanied by the low descent of the diaphragm, results in a phenomenon called "tracheal pull," where "the trachea exerts a pulling force on the larynx."[7] When this occurs, it reduces glottal adduction, which may help singers avoid "pressed phonation."[8] Although desirable in many styles of singing, a low inhalation strategy may counteract the greater vocal fold adduction that is necessary for belting.

Sundberg, along with researcher Jenny Iwarsson, additionally found that tracheal pull also lowers the larynx, thereby lengthening the vocal tract.[9] According to voice scientist Ingo R. Titze, lengthening the vocal tract will lower all the formant frequencies of the voice, resulting in a darker timbre.[10] This may not be what singers are looking for, however, when performing in genres that prioritize a more speech-based tone that favors brighter sound qualities.

As Benson also points out, there is a "ubiquitous presence of audio technology amplification" when singing in CCM genres.[11] When using microphones, singers may not need the same level of activity of the respiratory system as when producing unamplified tones that must be heard over an orchestra. These are just a few examples of how a slow and low inhalation that results in abdominal distension may not always be the most effective breathing strategy for singers.

One of the more impactful understandings that has influenced my teaching is that the vocal systems are nonlinear.[12] An intentionally simplistic explanation of a linear process, as it relates to voicing, is that breath flows up from the lungs, passes through the vibrating vocal folds, and the resulting sound is then enhanced in the vocal tract, shaped by the articulators, and sent out to the ears of the listeners. But the vocal systems actually behave in a nonlinear, interactive way. This means that changing any one of the vocal systems (respiration, phonation, resonance, articulation, etc.) can impact all the other systems, both upstream and downstream of where the change occurs. For instance, changing the shape of the vocal tract (in particular, to a more occluded position) will create a backflow of pressure that impacts the way the vocal folds vibrate together, potentially changing how much air is being released during phonation, and affecting how much air may be needed during inhalation. It may be that some singers have inefficiencies with the mechanics of breathing that could be leading to inefficiencies in their singing. But, for many vocal issues that were long considered to be rooted in the breath, the culprit (and the potential solution) may actually lie elsewhere.[13]

Lastly, there is some evidence that body type may have an influence on someone's breathing inclinations. Building on the research of Jeannette D. Hoit and Thomas J. Hixon,[14] voice pedagogue Jennifer Griffith Cowgill published a study in the *Journal of Singing* titled "Breathing for Singers: A Comparative Analysis of Body Types and Breathing Tendencies."[15] She found that singers with mesomorph body types (a muscular build with lower levels of body fat) displayed large amounts of rib cage and vertical chest movement with little movement in the abdominal area during respiration.

Ectomorphs (lean body types) had similar tendencies, but also displayed a high degree of movement in the lateral and vertical chest wall. By contrast, endomorphs (people with higher percentages of body fat) tended to have more movement in the thoracic and abdominal regions. As voice pedagogue Matthew Edwards highlights, perhaps the most notable parts of the study are the measurements of forced vital capacity (FVC), forced expiratory volume (FEV), FEV/FVC-percent, and peak flow. Results indicate no statistically significant difference in these measurements among the various breathing patterns. As Edwards concludes, "It is impossible to say that one type of expansion is universally better than the other."[16] This being the case, perhaps breathing for singing should be tailored toward what bodies do most naturally rather than being directed toward a supposed universal ideal.

All of this information has led to the idea that we should consider focusing less on breathing in the voice studio—just observe what students are doing most naturally and "if it ain't broke, don't fix it." We can obviously be mindful of releasing unnecessary tensions within the respiratory system, addressing imbalances of pressure, and encouraging the development of different breathing strategies for different tasks. But, if singers seem to be breathing sufficiently for the vocal tasks they are trying to accomplish, we may be better served by staying out of the way.

In this regard, Bob's approaches to breathing seem to reflect this understanding. Certainly, in my experience, he would discuss technical aspects of breathing as needed. However, there was no obsessive focus on respiratory mechanics, no hands on the belly insisting on a certain degree of abdominal expansion, and no claims that efficient breathing was the singular key to effective singing. Instead, his main emphasis was to allow the desire to communicate a specific idea to serve as the impetus (the "inspiration," as it were) for inhalation. More on that later.

Still, when pressed in our interviews, Bob offered more details about how he approached breathing for singing with new or beginning students in particular. "One of the first things that I check is if they are using the breath properly, because 'No air, no sound; no sound, no dollars,'" he said. "There's just no point in going to part B if they're not getting the air in and they're not getting the air out. If you don't have air in your body—in the lungs—under some amount of pressure, there's no way you're going to be able to sing. Pe-ri-od."

One of the more common inefficiencies Bob would often see in students—even advanced ones—was what he called, for lack of a better term, the "slouching chest." Although this is generally an issue of posture and alignment, it has the ability to negatively impact singing before a single tone is uttered.

He would often encourage a sense of the chest being high and wide, which he feels serves two purposes. "First, it allows you more air," he says. "Second, it also shows that you're comfortable in your own skin." He suspects the lack of the latter may have contributed to some of the less-than-ideal postures he saw in his voice studio. "Some of it may have been due to discomfort, maybe being somewhat intimidated being in the room with a teacher, perhaps for the first time. That's not an easy thing. So in the early stages of the lessons, particularly with young students, you had to constantly remind them about posture."

For one of the more stunning examples of posture and alignment—and being comfortable in one's own skin—he again recalls the recital given by Elizabeth Schwarzkopf. "When she walked out, her arms were actually somewhat behind her because of the expansion of the chest, rather than being caved in," he says. "Once again, by carrying herself the way she did, we knew she was in complete command of the evening."

The other respiratory inefficiency Bob often observed in young singers was constriction during inhalation. "I found the students, all too many times, were very practiced at 'taking' a breath, which I always thought was kind of a selfish way to approach breathing," he says. In our interview, he demonstrated by inhaling in a way that can best be described as a gasp or catch breath. When imitating the sound myself, I can feel narrowing and even tightness in the vocal tract. "Many times, that sort of breath was provoked by individuals who don't necessarily sing, like coaches or conductors," he says. Conductors are sometimes prone to using an audible breath to "help" the singers know when to come in. There is some evidence that singers will unwittingly imitate various movements, particularly during preparatory gestures, so it stands to reason that singers may subconsciously imitate constricted breathing if modeled by a conductor.[17]

Conductors weren't the only culprits, however. "It could even be from voice teachers who, through their directions, encouraged the least amount of time for the most important need, which is allowing an ample intake of air alongside the comfortable feeling of inhalation." Significantly for Bob, giving sufficient time for proper inhalation has the added benefit of allowing singers to use the act of breathing as part of their communication.

Just as the systems of singing can be mistakenly thought of in a linear manner—breath to phonation to resonance to articulation—artistic expression can also be thought to follow a linear process. In other words, singers inhale efficiently, then phonate effectively, then begin communicating the ideas they wish to express. Bob takes a different approach, advocating that breathing *is* communication. If singers are waiting until phonation to communicate, they are missing opportunities to engage the audience in the stories they are telling. "One of the best, least costly actions you can take in singing is to communicate without even having to sing a note—on inhalation," he says. "You get paid for it! Use that time of silence. Fill it with communication."

He further explains: "The purpose of breathing is to create physical comfort so that you can communicate fully and draw a listener into you. Actually, not so much into you, the singer, but into the text and the music, which is more important."

To this end, Bob finds that when singers breathe with a clear intention about what they are preparing to communicate, it accomplishes two things. First, in most cases, it will allow them to bring a sufficient amount of air into their bodies for the task they are about to undertake. Second, it allows the storytelling to continue, even when no voicing is occurring. "You're giving me a hint of what you are about to say during your inhalation," he says. "The breath can be a reflection of what you just said—essentially a postlude to what you said—or it can be a prelude to what you're about to say."

Breathing in such a way makes efficient use of singers' resources. "This is economical singing," Bob says. "Music is a language, and silence is just as important to communication as sound is. When you're free to use silence in your singing, by God, use it. No one's paying you extra to make more noise. They're paying you to be a communicative singer."

Often in lessons, Bob was accustomed to students expecting to be told exactly how to breathe for singing, likely because of how it has traditionally been emphasized in voice training. In an effort to go "from the known to the unknown," he would frequently return to a specific analogy:

"Imagine you've been asking your dad for years for a red Beamer. Well, one year, your dad earns an inheritance and comes into some money. He then elects to use some of that money to buy a nice gift for each of his children. So, you come downstairs on Christmas morning, not expecting this year to be any different than the others. But this time, you look out the window and you see a great big green bow on top of a brand-new red Beamer. Now, you don't have to check in with me to ask how you should inhale in a way that sufficiently conveys your presumed excitement to your father. You will show your father the genuine excitement you feel in your breathing and in your vocalization without having to disturb my Christmas morning."

The same visualization practice can be used in other instances when communicating song texts. "Go back and imagine your first experience with broken love," Bob suggests. "All of us have to go through that and it's very, very painful. How did you feel? How might you take a breath when you are experiencing that feeling? How might you color your voice? If you haven't had an experience like that to remember, imagine what it might feel like. You don't have to tell me in words what you've felt—that's personal. But, that's what you're singing about, so that's the message you have to convey."

"Taking" a Breath

One colleague Bob credits with influencing his approach to breathing for singing is author and pedagogue Shirlee Emmons (1923–2010). An artist and scholar, Emmons was awarded both the Marian Anderson Award and a Fulbright Scholarship. She served on the faculties of several universities over the course of her forty-six-year teaching career (including at Columbia University, Princeton University, and Boston University) and authored four books and numerous articles on singing. Like Bob, she also was born in Wisconsin, earning a bachelor's degree and later an honorary doctorate from Lawrence University.

"I greatly adored Shirlee," Bob says. "Still today, I find her to be one of the greatest teachers of my time." Emmons was particularly enthralled with the practices advocated by CU voice professor Berton Coffin, which she used heavily in her teaching. As Bob recalls, "It was to the point where she could say to a student, for instance, 'I want the Coffin exercise on page eighty-five of the red book.' But she did not misuse the book. Shirlee used it to create communicative singers."

One exercise he remembers seeing her use was asking students to do an elliptical movement with both arms, back and forth along the sides of their bodies. When the arms come back, the chest widens. She could then analyze the degree to which the chest seemed appropriately high and wide for each student, given their individual ranges of motion. When they reached that point, which was usually with the arms farther back than the students were used to, she would ask them to allow the arms to release and fall to the sides while still maintaining the high and wide chest position. Besides creating a greater area in which the lungs could expand when inhaling for singing, the students came away with a sensation of how that position felt compared to their habitual way of standing. Bob's reaction upon seeing the effectiveness of the exercise was immediate. "I thought, 'There's no simpler way.'"

Emmons would then draw students' attention to their lower torsos while they took slow inhalations in this new physical posture, allowing them to feel the freedom of movement in that area. As Bob describes, "I don't suppose I can *feel* a breath, technically speaking, because I can't feel my lungs. I'm not sure that the nerve endings in the lungs are fashioned in such a way that I can feel my lungs expand. What I feel when I breathe is the effect—the result—of the expansion of the lungs. The diaphragm is descending and everything beneath it is being pressed down upon. That creates the expansion." By helping students find space and freedom in the torso and abdomen, Bob believed that they were better able to discover the sensations associated with breathing. Those sensations then provided feelings they could remember and recreate when developing a consistent, individualized use of breath for singing.

As students recognized the ease with which breath could be brought into the body when it was uninhibited in this way, Bob would remind them that they did not have to "take" a breath at all. They merely needed to prepare the body in such a way that it was easily able to receive the air. "That's a whole hell of a lot less work than 'taking' a breath," he says.

Bob has similar misgivings about the phrase "catch breath." Used to describe rapid inhalations, it often occurs when the pace of the music being sung does not allow for a slower, more thorough inhalation. "It does exactly as it's titled—it stops the air from fully inflating the lungs," Bob says. "I don't know how many times I was told, 'Just take a catch breath.' I know I've said it, out of desperation." Instead, he believes that taking a longer inhalation creates a sense of peace within the singer, which is much more conducive to artistic expression than singing from a place of constriction as a result of employing catch breaths. "I'm not paid to take catch breaths. I'm being paid to fill up the lungs and feel comfortable about it," he says.

If the music does not give singers sufficient time to take such a breath, Bob believes they should simply insist upon it and do it anyway. "I was always an advocate of giving students permission to take as much time as necessary to breathe," he says. "Because if there's no air, there's no sound. And if there's no sound, you ain't gonna be paid for the gig! I used to tell the students, 'No one has the business or the right or the legal authority to tell you not to breathe. No one.' If you need to breathe in the middle of the word, make that negative into a positive, just like Aretha Franklin did, when she sang for Obama's inauguration—the first time. During the first line of 'My country 'tis of thee,' she took a breath in the middle of the word 'country,' and it worked wonderfully. She communicated with it. No one will ever fault you for taking a breath *if* it's a communicative breath."

Understanding that singers are wind instruments, Bob often found himself negotiating for more time for singers to breathe. "I had to argue and get a little feisty with pianists now and then because, for example, if you had a quarter rest, I wanted that to be a full quarter rest, if not slightly longer, so that a singer has time to allow breath into the lungs," he says.

But none of this attention to breath can be completed effectively if the body is not set up to receive air. "What I found myself having to repeat often is, 'Your chest is sinking. Let's go back.' If someone is going to sing a five-measure phrase, they're not going to do it well with a chest that's down around the knees," he says.

Notes

1. Giovanni Battista Lamperti as quoted in Barbara Draina, *The Breathing Book for Singers* (Flagstaff, AZ: Mountain Peak Music, 2019), i.
2. George Gagnidze as quoted in Brian Manternach, "George Gagnidze: Baritone Back in Business," *Classical Singer,* January/February 2022, 24–5.
3. Elizabeth Ann Benson, *Training Contemporary Commercial Singers* (Oxford: Compton Publishing Ltd., 2020), 110.
4. Ibid.
5. Leda Scearce, *Manual of Singing Voice Rehabilitation: A Practical Approach to Vocal Health and Wellness* (San Diego, CA: Plural Publishing, Inc., 2016), 162.

6   Ibid., 210.

7   Johan Sundberg, "Breathing Behavior during Singing," *The NATS Journal* 49, no. 3 (January/February 1993): 49.

8   Ibid., 50.

9   Jenny Iwarsson and Johan Sundberg, "Effects of Lung Volume on Vertical Larynx Position during Phonation," *Journal of Voice* 12, no. 2 (1998): 159–65.

10 Ingo R. Titze, *Principles of Voice Production* (Iowa City, IA: National Center for Voice and Speech, 2000), 179.

11 Benson, *Training Contemporary Commercial Singers*.

12 This concept is explained in greater detail in Ingo R. Titze, "The Language and Basic Phenomena of Nonlinear Dynamics in Vocal Fold Vibration," *Journal of Singing* 76, no. 3 (January/February 2020): 295–7.

13 As described by pedagogue Nicholas Perna in the *VocalFri* podcast, "If you want to sing a longer phrase, you need to phonate efficiently. And if you are not phonating efficiently, you will not sing longer phrases. . . . Let's just say you already have breathy phonation and you just put more exhalatory force against the vocal folds, and all you're doing is blowing more air through a flabby glottis. Is that helpful? . . . Let's say it was pressed phonation and all you're doing is blowing more air against already pressed phonation. Is that going to be helpful? . . . One of the other ways to fix phonation is, of course, to go one step further down the track and actually fix the resonance shape with the articulatory system and give yourself some good feedback acoustically with the shape of the vocal tract, which can also encourage good flow phonation. So, in other words, your resonator itself can fix your phonator." Nicholas Perna and Sarah Pigott, "The Breathing Episode," *VocalFri Podcast*, September 26, 2019, 29:18–34:49, https://www.vocalfri.com/e/the-breathing-episode/.

14 Jeannette D. Hoit and Thomas J. Hixon, "BodyType and Speech Breathing," *Journal of Speech and Hearing Research* 29, no. 3 (September 1986): 313–24.

15 Jennifer Griffith Cowgill, "Breathing for Singers: A Comparative Analysis of Body Types and Breathing Tendencies," *Journal of Singing* 66, no. 2 (November/December 2009): 141–7.

16 Matthew Edwards, "Mix It Up Monday: Thinking about Body Type and Age When Teaching Breath Management," November 6, 2017, https://edwardsvoice.wordpress.com/2017/11/06/mix-it-up-monday-thinking-about-body-type-and-age-when-teaching-breath-management/ (accessed April 6, 2024).

17 Jeremy N. Manternach, "Effects of Varied Conductor Prep Movements on Singer Muscle Engagement and Voicing Behaviors," *Psychology of Music* 44, no. 3 (2016): 574–86. doi: 10.1177/0305735615580357; Jeremy N. Manternach, "The Effect of Varied Conductor Preparatory Gestures on Singer Upper Body Movement," *Journal of Music Teacher Education* 22, no. 1 (2012): 20–34. doi: 10.1177/1057083711414428.

9 Balanced Phonation
SOVTEs, Negotiating the *Passaggio*, and Exercising the Whole Voice

Once sufficient air has been taken in for the task at hand, Bob believes that phonation should initiate with a balance of air pressure and airflow. In seeking this with student singers, he would often ask them to begin on an [m] hum. "I learned that from Jean Westerman Gregg, who was a former president of NATS and the daughter of Kenneth Westerman [author of *Emergent Voice*]," Bob says.[1]

Singing on nasal consonants is ubiquitous in voice training, but Bob had specific reasons for favoring them. First of all, it is easily accomplished by most students—"There probably aren't many individuals who can't do an [m] hum." Second, it engages the vocal folds in a way that encourages balanced phonation. As he says, "Starting with an [m] hum, if done properly, gets the edges of the vocal folds to vibrate, if you're not over-pressurizing."

Additionally, Bob believed the [m] hum helped students avoid glottal onsets, where air pressure builds up below closed vocal folds before vocalization. "I don't find glottal attacks to be bad," he clarifies. "I was taught in all my pedagogy courses that they're terrible and they should never be used. But, we speak with glottal attacks all the time. 'I' has a glottal attack, for instance. I haven't been sent to the laryngologist's office yet for using glottal attacks in my speaking. On the other hand, if it's a heavy glottal attack, of course, those we want to throw out."

Bob had a unique way of directing students to perform the [m] hum. "I would often ask students to blow a little bit of air through the nostrils first before vocalizing the [m]. That way the vocal folds would engage more automatically as a result of the airflow that creates the vacuum that brings the folds together." Bob would use that exercise with students in the middle voice, then lower middle voice, and then the upper middle voice.

Once singers had primed the middle ranges with the [m] hum, he would generally move on to lip trills, starting again in the middle voice but then extending up to the top range and down to the singers' lowest notes. He was particularly fond of the lip trill because of its ability to establish balance between air pressure and airflow. But he also liked the exercise because of how it could draw singers' attention to their respiratory systems. "During lip trills, I wanted to bring singers back to their breathing and get them to feel that wonderful resistance of pressure building up in the mid area," he says. "If I felt that I was hearing too much pressure in the voice, I would mention that and we would change it, maybe by releasing a little bit of air before the lip trill. I don't think there's any mystery—too much pressure is because of too little airflow; the lack of pressure is due to too much airflow."

Flow Phonation and SOVTEs

There are similarities in Bob's approach of managing air pressure and airflow to the concept of "flow phonation." As Titze describes, flow phonation "feels effortless and efficient because ample airflow is passed through the glottis when the vocal folds vibrate."[2] He uses the analogy of water flowing from a reservoir, where the valve can be opened or closed by degrees to release more or less water. In a similar way, the vocal folds can be abducted to increase airflow or adducted to decrease airflow until the right balance is established. Importantly, as Titze points out, "every singing teacher and speech-language pathologist knows that excessive flow makes the voice breathy and weak. It is therefore a question of optimizing the airflow, not maximizing it."[3]

In Sundberg's description of flow phonation, he notes that there is "a minimal degree of vocal fold adduction, just so much that the vocal folds barely make contact during the closed phase of the vibratory cycle." This aligns with Bob's idea of allowing just the edges of the vocal folds to vibrate at the start of sound. Sundberg believes flow phonation helps singers avoid pressed phonation, which, from Bob's perspective, would keep the voice from being overly pressurized.

For more than two decades, voice scientists and voice pedagogues have been thoroughly researching the efficacy of semi-occluded vocal tract exercises (SOVTEs)—like the [m] hum and lip trills. In short, an SOVTE is any vocal exercise that partially blocks a portion of the vocal tract, either continuously or intermittently. There are many types of SOVTEs, including singing into straws of various lengths and diameters, singing on voiced fricative consonants (like [v] and [z]), and singing on nasal consonants (including [n] and [ŋ], as well as [m]).

Titze has published extensively on the effects of SOVTEs on vocalization, and has inspired a generation of voice researchers to further explore the benefits these exercises have in both singing training and voice rehabilitation. Among the primary benefits he notes are how SOVTEs "square up" the top edges of the vocal folds, positioning them for coordinated vibration.[4] SOVTEs can also lower phonation threshold pressure, meaning they reduce the amount of effort required to initiate sound.[5] They also tend to reduce any excessive vocal fold collision force that may lead to vocal fatigue.[6] Finally, they allow singers to "stretch and unpress" the vocal folds, which facilitates balanced phonation, especially when singing in higher ranges or through register transition points (*passaggi*).

I don't know how familiar Bob was during his teaching years with the term "semi-occluded vocal tract exercises" or the research that has been done on their effectiveness. The fact that much of the information on these exercises has really only become widely known among singing teachers in the years after his retirement leads me to believe that "SOVTE" was not part of his lexicon, though it was certainly part of his practice. Suffice it to say that his use of nasal consonants and lip trills, and his reasons for using them in the voice studio, aligns with modern research.

Passing through the Narrow Hallway

Once students' voices had been sufficiently warmed up and balanced phonation had been established, Bob would move on to exercises designed to address the specific needs of each individual singer. One of the issues that would undoubtedly need to be addressed in most tenor, baritone, and bass voices was the negotiation of the *passaggio*. Bob remembers Barbara Doscher referring to that process as, "coming through the narrow hallway." Bob adds, "We've got to be really careful coming through that passaggio. It's so damn narrow that, if there's wet paint on either wall, it's easy to rub our elbows in it."

As he points out, much of the trouble that tenors, baritones, and basses experience with the passaggio happens as a result of testosterone's influence on the voice, whether this occurs during puberty or when taken at a later age as part of testosterone therapy. In the first case, the laryngeal cartilages grow, and the vocal folds lengthen and thicken. In the second case, although there are individual differences, the laryngeal cartilages do not grow in the same way, but the vocal folds still generally thicken, resulting in a significant drop in pitch. When these changes are new, the voice can often feel cumbersome and heavy and may lack the flexibility it once had.

Bob recalls the personal disappointment he experienced with his own singing voice when he went through puberty. "It cost me my soprano voice. That was hard to lose," he says. Besides the loss of high notes, the limited voice that remained after the big shift downward was also disappointing. "I realized that I had become what I would later call an 'eight-note singer.' I had about eight notes that were good and the rest of them were poop," he says.

Although issues related to navigating the passaggio are quite common, not every singer Bob worked with struggled in this area. He often found that the higher the voice, the higher the passaggio would lie, and the less difficulty those singers would have when transitioning registers. He notes one former student who practically appeared not to have a passaggio at all. "Yes, it was there, but you didn't hear it. It was inaudible," he says. "Working with him, I didn't have to fuss a whole lot about the passaggio."

For most other tenors, however, this area of the voice required significant focus. Bob's favorite exercise to start blending the registers was to start with a pure falsetto [u] on a descending scale. In order to initially prevent students from being tempted to "mix" the note too high in the range, he would sometimes have them start with a puff of air by adding an "h" to the start of the exercise. Once they got to approximately F_4, he would encourage them to start mixing by changing the vowel from [u] to [ʊ] (as in "hook") as they continued to descend. Over time, he found that these falsetto exercises would help lead to successful transitioning from the upper register to the middle voice. "Young teachers, including myself, were always disappointed if that exercise didn't fix the issue the first time," he says. "How loony! But by training the muscles over a period of time, the change occurred."

Bob would often use the same exercise successfully with baritones and basses. However, due to the lower-lying passaggio in these voices, he would ask for the shift from falsetto to mix to occur at E_4 or possibly E-flat$_4$. "But again, you have to listen," he says. "If the voice sits a little lower, it may have to shift at D." He would sometimes consult Coffin's acoustic charts to find which vowels may be most facilitated in that part of the range, but he would always trust his ears to see if that recommendation was appropriate for individual students.

Top to Bottom

Bob was also an advocate of exercising the full range of all voices, regardless of voice type. "I always thought, just because you're a tenor, or just because you're a coloratura, you still have to be able to sing below the staff, if possible," he says. "We aren't just training the top voice, we're training the whole voice. Every once in a while, you may need those notes." He highlights how some of the most commonly performed literature requires a wide vocal range. "For example, in *Dichterliebe*, there's a low A," he says. "Even if you're singing it in the high key, you're going to need that low A."

The same philosophy applies to lower voices and their top ranges. "The mezzos in my studio, for example, if the voice would allow, they could sing a high C," he says. "Not that they would necessarily use that on stage. But because they could vocalize to a high C, or a high C-sharp, or a high D, knowing that they can sing those pitches gives them the ease to sing an A-flat, A, or B-flat. But the whole voice has to be vocalized."

Notes

1 Kenneth N. Westerman, *Emergent Voice* (Ann Arbor, MI: Self-published, 1947).
2 Ingo R. Titze, "On Flow Phonation and Airflow Management," *Journal of Singing* 72, no. 1 (September/October 2015): 57.
3 Ibid.
4 Karin Titze Cox and Ingo R. Titze, *Voice Is Free After SOVT* (Clearfield, UT: National Center for Voice and Speech, 2023), 58.
5 Ingo R. Titze, "Voice Training and Therapy with a Semioccluded Vocal Tract: Rationale and Scientific Underpinnings," *Journal of Speech, Language, and Hearing Research* 49, no. 2 (April 2006): 448–59, https://doi.org/10.1044/1092-4388(2006/035).
6 Ibid.

10 A Vowel-Based Approach to Resonance
Assessing Pressure versus Flow

Many of Bob's other approaches to establishing balance in the voice were based on his understanding of close vowels (sometimes referred to as "closed vowels") as being more "pressurized" than open vowels. Although the tactics he used achieved positive results, I suspect their effectiveness may not be due to the reasons he believed. It seems to me that if a process leads to improvement, we should follow that process, even if we don't know exactly why it works or happen to be mistaken as to why it works. Below, Bob describes how he used vowels to address what he identified as issues with pressure versus flow. I will then add my own thoughts as to what may have contributed to the success of these tactics.

Bob recalls his first exposure to the idea of certain vowels creating more pressure than others, which came about while observing Doscher teach. "I said, 'Barbara, you talk pressure and flow, but you don't seem to correct it by going where I think you should probably go—to the breathing machine.' She pulled her glasses down and said, 'Oh, Bob, you know better than that. An [ɑ] vowel releases pressure. An [i] vowel creates pressure. That's why we don't want sopranos singing [i] on high C-sharp.'"

In further observations, Bob found that both Berton Coffin and Shirlee Emmons advocated a similar approach to Doscher's. He found additional reinforcement when he read *Emergent Voice* by Kenneth Westerman, which provided considerable clarity for him regarding how the articulatory system influences the vocal folds. "In terms of technique, it often comes down to whether there is too much pressure or whether there is too much airflow. If there's too much pressure, then I've got to open the valve—the resonance valve, that is, not the vocal fold valve," he says. "That was a 'Wow!' when I realized that. I thought, 'Why didn't people tell me that before?'"

From that point forward, he was constantly monitoring what he perceived to be the needed balance between air pressure and airflow in singers, though he rarely used words like "pressure" in voice lessons. He simply had them adjust the vowel they were singing. "Let's say a soprano had to sing an [i] vowel on E_5 and I felt it was a little screechy and did not match the meaning of the text," he says. "I would ask her to think about releasing the air by giving her a back vowel, or as Kenneth Westerman called them, breathing vowels—an [u]. By giving her a back vowel (or a breathing vowel, or whatever you want to call them), that would release the air and cut down the pressure." In this way, he relied on singers' abilities to adjust vowels, without necessarily changing them completely. "If an [i] vowel is written, you owe it to the composer and you owe it to the poet to sing an [i] vowel, even if it's set on a pitch where [i] is not particularly easy to sing," he says. "So I'll help you by giving you a little bit of [u] articulation to release some of the air while the tongue is still, for the most part, in an [i] position. And now you can have your cake and eat it, too."

When Bob was at the University of Colorado, he frequently found scores in the music library with Doscher's markings in them from previous voice lessons. If she felt a vowel would require a little more [u], she would mark it in the score. He notes how Doscher would often advocate that singers use a combination of vowels, which she would indicate by writing a front vowel and a back vowel separated by a slash. "You would never sing a front vowel without some back vowel, and she'd give you that pairing," he says.

A related strategy Bob used was to simply have singers create more of an opening at the jaw. "If you had someone who was overpressuring the top, you could see if they can drop the jaw just a little bit, even while performing a lip trill or tongue trill," he says. "That's an articulation for air movement. What you want to do is move them away from a mouth position and tongue position that is going to create breath pressure and instead move them into an air movement posture. Anytime the jaw drops, the air is allowed to move more freely."

He would occasionally be interrupted in voice lessons, particularly by graduate students, who would cite some of the more prominently published pedagogues, saying, "Now, Vennard said . . ." or "But, Coffin said . . ." His response was usually some form of, "I know. But it's not about Coffin right now. It's about Heine and Schumann, the poet and the composer. We are, however, going to use Coffin's work to see if we can find a way that the composer and the poet can have that [i] without you feeling strangled singing it."

Bob allowed for the possibility that his understanding of how this approach works may have been incomplete. "I don't know to what extent some of this information has been countered in this day and age now, because there's been a great deal of change and growth in voice science—rightfully so," he says. "But that's what I learned through Coffin, and it still makes sense to me."

Acoustic Considerations

Some of what may be missing in Bob's descriptions is the acoustic component. Although a detailed discussion of vocal acoustics is beyond the scope of this book, a few elements may be worth noting.[1] Specifically, we can look at what happens acoustically when vowels are adjusted.

During voicing, when a harmonic of the pitch being sung (fundamental frequency) aligns with a vocal tract resonance, it receives a boost in intensity (amplitude).[2] These resonances shift location depending on the vowel being sung. An [i] vowel, for instance, has a relatively low first resonance (generally in the area of 300 Hz) and a comparatively high second resonance (generally in the area of 2,500 Hz). The aforementioned high C-sharp (C-sharp$_6$) has a fundamental frequency of 1,108 Hz, which lies well above the location of the first resonance of the [i] vowel and well below its second resonance. Therefore, to try to articulate a pure [i] on a C-sharp$_6$ would prove challenging, if not impossible. In this scenario, a slight adjustment would bring the second harmonic ($2f_o$) in line with the second resonance, resulting in a timbre that is brighter than what is typically called for from sopranos in Western classical singing, where the fundamental carries most of the acoustic energy. The [ɑ] vowel, however, has a first resonance location that generally ranges between 800 and 1,200 Hz and a second resonance that generally ranges between 1,100 and 1,500 Hz. Therefore, with more subtle adjustments, the fundamental frequency of C-sharp$_6$ is more likely to align with one of the resonances of [ɑ]. In which case, the reason "we don't want sopranos singing [i] on high C-sharp" may be due to acoustic considerations rather than an issue of pressure versus flow.

Concerning the example of a soprano singing a "screechy" E_5, the vowels [i] and [u] have similar first resonance locations. The second resonance of [u], however, is much lower than that of [i]—usually well below 1,000 Hz. The high second resonance, along with the higher location of all subsequent resonances, is what gives [i] its characteristic brightness. When "adding some [u]" in a sung [i] vowel, likely by rounding the lips, the second resonance and all subsequent resonances lower, highlighting lower frequencies and adding more of the characteristic warmth of [u] to the sound. This may help avoid any perceived screechiness when singing an [i].

Bob also mentions lowering the jaw as "an articulation for air movement." Lowering the jaw will also raise the location of the first resonance of a vowel.[3] As Titze states, by adjusting vowels and degrees of jaw opening, singers "can use the vocal tract for intensity regulation," which may be internally perceived as changes in pressure and flow.[4]

Since Bob identifies the regulator of pressure as "the resonance valve" and not "the vocal fold valve," he seems to be specifically referring to supraglottic/intraoral pressure, which *can* influence timbre. However, what he is hearing and describing are more likely timbral shifts due to changing balances in acoustic energy distribution. Of course, there are instruments available today that are used in voice research and in clinical settings that can measure elements like airflow and degree of vocal fold closure during vocalization, which may be able to confirm or challenge Bob's strategies and the results they are intended to bring about. The only tools Bob would implement in his assessments of pressure and flow, however, were his ears. "I don't have a meter to control or show me those pressure levels, but I know I can hear it," he says. "This goes back, again, to the importance of listening. Scientists may be able to measure those things, but I didn't need to talk about that in lessons because it was so far removed from a young student's understanding. I can't say, 'Give me two more PSI.' But I can say, 'Give me more [i].' That's something they know and understand—going from the known to the unknown."

Agility, Dynamics, and *Chiaroscuro*

Bob found that this vowel-based approach had many applications. When addressing agility, for example, he would work from a more pressurized vowel to a less pressurized one. "If I noticed that the singer was not able to demonstrate much, if any, facility—agility—generally, that was due to pressure," he says. "I would loosen the pressure by opening up the vowel little by little." He would intentionally start them on an [i] vowel to see how they would navigate a melismatic passage and mitigate the pressure. He would then progressively move them to more open vowels. He notes how many passages of *fioratura*, specifically in Rossini's music, are performed on open vowels. Once again, in approaching these sorts of passages, he returns to a familiar mantra. "I don't think there's any mystery. Pressure is because of too little airflow; the lack of pressure is because of too much airflow," he says.

Sometimes, before he could make an accurate assessment of a student's agility, he would have to pare an exercise down in order to find where the student could already experience a degree of success. Beginning with a short five-note scale, he would gradually work up to an octave or a nine-note scale and then up to two octave scales. But if the students started running into problems, he would shorten the exercise back down and focus once again on vowels.

This approach applies equally well to the shifts in dynamics necessary for accomplishing an effective *messa di voce*—a crescendo and decrescendo performed on a single note. Considered by many pedagogues to be one of the most difficult vocal exercises to execute, Bob highlights how vowels can facilitate, or interfere with, the task. "A decrescendo is done through vowels, in my book," he says. "If you want to create a messa di voce, if you want to go from loud to soft, you're going to be more open for the *forte* and more closed for the *pianissimo*. And in doing that, you are going from an air movement posture to one that creates more pressure. I don't see how anybody can sing softly and create a sound that will project when the mouth is wide open. So the messa di voce is controlled by the opening and closing of the valve—again, the resonance valve, not the vocal fold valve."

When directing students to consciously adjust vowels and mouth positions, Bob tended to avoid biomechanical instructions—in other words, instructions that involved direct manipulation of specific parts of the vocal anatomy. "Many times, in my early days of teaching, I would say, 'Can you elevate the tongue?' I could usually get away with that with an advanced student. But a beginning student might not have great sensitivity to the rise and the fall of the tongue."

This was another lesson he learned from Barbara Doscher. When he was at the University of Colorado, she taught all the vocal pedagogy courses, so he knew that his voice students who had been through her classes would be well-versed in the particulars of anatomy, physiology, and acoustics. Even so, the language she used in her voice studio differed from what she used in pedagogy classes. "Doscher never talked technically in voice lessons, unless it was absolutely necessary," Bob says. "If it was something that would aid the students' understanding, or if she knew it was absolutely relevant in giving them the ability to be able to change more quickly, then she might use that language. But what she never would do was mire them down in information that really wasn't going to speed up learning."

Bob followed her lead by focusing on changes in vowels rather than specific positioning of the articulators. These directions sometimes involved performing combinations of vowels or having a singer start with one vowel shape and gradually move in the direction of another. "I would ask beginners to sing an [ɑ] and slowly change the mouth position to an [u], saying nothing about the tongue position," he says. "If students then had difficulty with [u] because the tongue was backing, I would ask them to try to mix some [i] with the [u] to see if they could articulate them simultaneously. What we would often get is an umlaut, and that's okay, initially. Yes, that may lead them to mispronounce certain words, but it could be used as an exercise, as a means to an end. That's the glory of umlauts—you can teach fronting of the tongue while dealing with a back/open vowel."

Bob found the converse of this strategy to work, as well. "Let's say the vowels are too closed. Perhaps the word they are singing calls for an [i] but they're over-fronting the tongue. I would then ask them to articulate the [i] with some [u]. You may have to go to an [o] if you can't get it low enough. You may even have to go to an [ɑ] to get it. In most cases, the tongue is going to respond to that direction."

By subtly tweaking vowels in this way, Bob found that singers could attain the full yet balanced sound appropriate for classical and operatic styles. "The quality of the singing voice should have the highs, mediums, and lows—what's called the full orchestral sound of the voice," he says. "I think all singers have their own sound stamp, but it should have both bright and dark, the *chiaro* and the *oscuro*. As Shirlee Emmons would say, 'An [ɑ] should have some corners.' It shouldn't be one without the other. There may be times as a performer when you might choose a pure [i] or a pure [ɑ] to make your point, depending upon what you intend to say with the text. That's different. But the perfect sound within each one of us can be found when it has both the chiaro and the oscuro. That's home base."

Bob believes that this balance of timbre, created through a focus on vowels and resonance, encourages singers to incorporate greater degrees of freedom rather than trying to consciously control their sound with breath pressure, attempting to manipulate individual muscles, or placing an inordinate amount of focus on the larynx. "To sing with the greatest control, you have to give up the unnecessary controls," he says. "That will pay off in spades when it comes to communication."

Notes

1 For a more in-depth discussion of acoustics, see Ingo R. Titze's *Principles of Voice Production* (Iowa City, IA: National Center for Voice and Speech, 2000) and Kenneth W. Bozeman's *Practical Vocal Acoustics* (Lanham, MD: Rowman & Littlefield, 2022).
2 Although there are differences between fundamental frequency (f_o) and pitch, we can consider them to be equivalent for our purposes here.
3 Titze, *Principles of Voice Production*, 180, 257–8.
4 Ibid., 259.

11 Choosing Purposeful Exercises

Listening as the First Step to Problem-Solving

In going from the known to the unknown, Bob felt it was important to be flexible with his teaching and willing to adjust his approach based on the needs of the individual students he saw. Therefore, he was not an advocate of running through a fixed set of vocalizes with every singer. He feared that teachers who default to, as he says, "just doing a battery of meaningless exercises" may not truly be listening to their students in a way that can help target their specific needs.

He once read an article by a well-known opera singer who presented a list of the ten vocal exercises he uses in his own practice. Bob recalls thinking, "Okay, those exercises work for you. But are they going to work for every singer?" He felt that the implication of the article was that those ten exercises were all any singer would ever need to find success. Instead, Bob feels that teachers should work to provide more personalized instruction based on what each student displays, focusing on the areas they most need to develop. "I can't imagine anything more fraudulent in this business than telling singers, 'These are the ten exercises you should do,' without giving a reason for them, and then telling them they're ready to go," he says.

In 2002, Bob was selected as a master teacher for the intern program sponsored by the National Association of Teachers of Singing. (Though Bob was recognized by many as a "master teacher," he never embraced that title. "That's a really foolish term," he says. "I'm just a teacher. I'm being paid for what I'm doing, so I'm going to do my job to the best of my ability.") In this mentoring role, he observed a group of early-career teachers as they worked with a cohort of students. The young teachers would then receive feedback and guidance from the mentors on how to improve the effectiveness of their teaching. He was sometimes called upon to serve in a similar capacity for the IU student chapter of NATS, which hosted its own events modeled after the NATS Intern Program. In this version, graduate students at IU had the opportunity to teach undergraduate students in a master class setting in the presence of a more experienced teacher who offered advice on developing their skills as teachers. In these workshops, Bob found that nearly every student whom he supervised would ask him some variation of the same question at the start of their teaching lesson: "Dr. Harrison, where do I begin?" "That's sad," Bob says. "Horrifically sad. I couldn't imagine feeling so unprepared. And my somewhat nasty, I suppose, response was, 'Have you ever thought of listening? Why don't we start there?'"

He is critical of teachers who come to lessons with a set agenda, putting the students through a certain predetermined set of paces, regardless of what sounds the students happen to be making in any given lesson. "From my very first day as a teacher, I knew that I should be listening to the student in front of me and reacting to that," he says. "I knew what I was listening for, which would then be the goal of my instruction. So, what I had to teach in these workshops was for them to listen."

Whenever he saw this list-driven approach in student teachers he mentored, he asked, "What are you wanting to get out of this singer?" He recalls, "They would reply, 'I don't know. I'm just doing the exercises that so-and-so gave to me.'" Incredulous, Bob often responded, "Well, this student isn't paying for that."

"I've got a little list . . . "

Full disclosure: I have a list of vocal exercises that I give to my students. (Sorry, Bob!) That being said, I agree that handing out such a list without an explanation of the purpose of each exercise is limited in its usefulness. However, when students do have an understanding of what each exercise is designed to facilitate, I find that it encourages mindful, self-directed practice sessions. The list, which I have titled Voice-building Exercises for Independent Practice, divides vocalizes into various categories such as agility, negotiating passaggio, resonance balancing, extending upper range, and so on. Of course, any grouping of notes (scales, arpeggios, etc.) can serve a variety of purposes, as long as they are performed with a specific intention in mind. But I have tried to include patterns of notes that would seem most likely to lead to the desired improvement for each voice-building category.

Rather than handing over the sheet and sending them off to the practice room, I work through the exercises with students in lessons so they have a clear understanding of how they may be performed efficiently and effectively for the stated purpose. This is especially beneficial when students take the time in their practice sessions to sing, assess, fine-tune, and repeat, as needed.

For each exercise, I also include at least one variation—using a different vowel, switching the order of the vowels used, incorporating a different SOVTE, and so on. This helps prevent the exercises from getting monotonous, but also moves away from "blocked practice" and in the direction of "variable practice," which may enhance learning, as spelled out by author and pedagogue John Nix.[1]

I find that categorizing the exercises according to the element of technique they are designed to address allows singers to prioritize their individualized technical goals in practice sessions. By gradually working through the full sheet of exercises, even if it takes multiple practice sessions to get through the entire list, singers will ensure that they are also giving attention to many other aspects of their technique. This will help them build a well-balanced instrument, even if they give more specialized attention to the parts of their technique they are most interested in developing. In the same way, someone who goes to the gym with the primary goal of developing big shoulders and biceps would likely be encouraged by a personal trainer to exercise the full body for optimal balance and function (even if shoulder and bicep exercises are prioritized).

One other list I sometimes draw from is Ingo Titze's "The Five Best Vocal Warm-up Exercises," which appears in the January 2001 issue of the *Journal of Singing*.[2] I appreciate how Titze lists the exercises, explains how to perform them, and then includes a "what is accomplished" pedagogical rationale for each one. When I share this article, I point out to students that the word "best" is right there in the title, so readers know immediately that there is a subjective nature to the article. Because of this, some students may not be drawn to every single exercise. But, because the rationale has been provided, teachers and students can work together to devise alternate exercises that may accomplish the same goals.[3]

Therefore, lists of vocalizes need not be summarily dismissed. Bob's point is well taken that just because a successful singer posts a list of preferred exercises does not mean any other singer who follows those exercises will achieve similar success. Even the lists of vocalizes I mention above may not lead to the intended results if they are handed out without explanation or demonstration, or if they do not address the specific technical needs or desires of individual students.

The alternative approach to following a list of vocal exercises, as Bob says, is to actively listen to each student, which he feels is the root of engaged teaching. "That's what it's about: listening, and then having some idea of anatomy and physiology, and coupling those two with an understanding of acoustics. Then asking yourself, is it a good sound? Is it a healthy sound? Is it a sound with which the singer can communicate properly and come out of a performance with two vocal folds that are still in good shape?" he says. "All of my problem-solving was based upon what I heard rather than going through a battery of exercises for no reason at all."

Bob believes that effective listening skills are the most crucial tools voice teachers must work toward developing—a strong belief, which Barbara Doscher drilled and cemented into his head. The more quickly and accurately teachers can hear inefficiencies, the more effectively they can use their time in voice lessons. This need is highlighted by some statistics that Bob calculated during his time at CU relating to those who teach in academic institutions. Assuming a 15-week semester and weekly 60-minute lessons, students meet one-on-one with their voice teachers for 30 hours each year, which amounts to 120 hours over a four-year degree program. When divided by 24 hours in each day, this breaks down to just five full days of time together. "That's all we get to see them," he says. "We've got only five days over their four years. I realized then that we have to get to it. We have to be able to quickly give a student the technique to make these corrections. Overall, I think students appreciate the approach of moving quickly, whether they realize or not exactly what is happening in the moment. I have to say, 'Here's what I hear and this is how I believe you should change it.'"

Barbara Doscher modeled for Bob the importance of listening as the first order of business for a voice teacher. He still recognizes this as one of her greatest skills—not only her ability to assess her students' singing but also how she helped them develop their own self-diagnosis skills. "She gave her students no choice but to listen," he says. "They had to listen to their own singing and they had to listen to the singing of others. And she would direct their listening as master piano tuners develop their practice, which depends on developing an acute set of ears."

Incidentally, Doscher also reinforced the idea that the primary purpose of a well-developed technique is to expressively serve the music. Bob recalls, "She used to say, 'What are we going to do once we get on the resonance? Is that it? No. Now the fun begins.'"

Due in part to these shared philosophies, and knowing Doscher played a pivotal role in his initial hiring at CU, Bob fondly remembers some meaningful compliments she paid him early in his career. "You know, Bob," he recalls her saying, "when you interviewed, you didn't have a clue. But I saw that you have some of the best listening skills I've ever seen in anyone, and you have a really high sense of inquiry. You will put in the time and effort to be an outstanding teacher." Bob took those comments to heart. "I was so profoundly taken by her teaching," he says.

Informed Listening

Upon reflection, Bob recognizes how much he has learned from simply being willing to pay attention and listen. This includes listening to his teachers, listening to music, and listening to the world around him. "I was thinking the other day about the teachers in my life—from grade school on up—who worked with me, gave me their time, and contributed to shaping me," he says. "And then I thought about those who taught me through their performances. Some of the greatest lessons I ever had were spent simply listening, which is not done enough now, I believe."

Bob feels that one of the best ways teachers can train themselves to know what to listen for in lessons is to actively listen to as many celebrated singers as possible. There is no limit to how many listening hours should be logged, since there is always something more to be gained. "As teachers of singing, we have to have listened to a great deal of music before we should even approach the profession. I find—and I think I probably share some responsibility in this occurring—if there's any hole in the current generation of voice teaching, it's that few teachers have listened to enough music and listened to great singers to even know what to teach," he says, adding, "Take that as my opinion. I'm sure it can be disputed."

Students may be further encouraged to seek out live recordings whenever possible. Knowing the "magic" that can occur in recording studio production, live recordings can give a more accurate reflection of singers' actual choices, both technical and artistic.

When listening to vocal music, singers should also be mindful that they are not giving all their focus to the vocal line. Of course, this is necessary for analyzing a singer's vocal technique, but for learning expressivity, artistry, and what makes a piece "art music," they must take in the entirety of the work.

Similarly, Bob believes they should not limit their listening to strictly vocal music. There is much to be gained from delving into the instrumental music of great composers and paying attention to how professional-level instrumentalists, for instance, shape a phrase, articulate, and approach dynamics.

As a Milton College undergraduate student at his professor's listening parties, Bob discovered that a key to the learning experience of listening is the elimination of distractions—an increasingly difficult task in today's device-laden culture. Lynn Helding highlights that attention is a necessary component of learning, which makes it appropriate that we use the phrase "*pay* attention." Once again, in *The Musician's Mind*, she states, "We have to want to learn, to pay attention. This very fact is embedded in the use of the word *pay*, which reflects our fund of attention and implies that learning costs us something."[4] Our increasing attachment to technology constantly divides our attention, and advertisers use this to their advantage, knowing that when they convince us to succumb and click the bait, their companies stand to profit. When we give our attention to these distractions, we have less mental capital to give to other matters, even those we claim to value. Therefore, undistracted listening is crucial for learning, for taking in the full scope of a piece of music, and for training our capacity to focus attention in one area for long periods of time.

It is difficult for Bob to overemphasize the importance of focused, critical listening, done with a spirit of curiosity and an attention to detail. For both singers and teachers of singing, he believes it is a necessary task that, when regularly practiced, can reap untold benefits. "Listening is what shaped me," he says. "I will go to my grave believing that."

In addition to listening to music, Bob feels that singers should immerse themselves in stories, constantly exploring the way words on a page can reflect the highs and lows of life. They should be encouraged to seek out creative literature, especially when it includes characters whose experiences are different from their own. All of this helps to build imagination and better equip singers to communicate with empathy, even when relating experiences they have not lived through themselves.

Bob recalls a story his CU colleague, pianist and conductor Robert Spillman, shared with him. One year, when Spillman was teaching at the Aspen Music Festival, a famed mezzo-soprano was working in a master class with a student singer. As the session went on, she was becoming exasperated with the lack of results she was getting from the student and the seeming dearth of imagination the student was displaying. After continued bewilderment, she is said to have remarked, "You need to read more." The student earnestly asked, "Which book?"

While acknowledging the humor in that story, the reality is that we cannot expect young students to have the personal life experience to truly know all the joys and tragedies that are conveyed through music. The next best thing, Bob believes, is to read about the experiences of others. In this way, students can have surrogate experiences to connect with, whether those are feelings of love, devastation, loss, euphoria, or any other emotions that come as we log more years on earth. "You can learn those things by reading accounts in books," Bob says. "Which book? This student had no idea where to begin."

Notes

1 John Nix, "Best Practices: Using Exercise Physiology and Motor Learning Principles in the Teaching Studio and the Practice Room," *Journal of Singing* 74, no. 2 (November/December 2017): 215–20.

2 Ingo R. Titze, "The Five Best Vocal Warm-up Exercises," *Journal of Singing* 57, no. 3 (January/February 2001): 51–2.

3 Other notable resources that offer vocal exercises alongside pedagogical rationale are Marci Rosenberg and Wendy D. LeBorgne's *The Vocal Athlete: Application and Technique for the Hybrid Singer*, 3rd ed. (San Diego, CA: Plural Publishing, 2024) and Kari Ragan's *A Systematic Approach to Voice: The Art of Studio Application* (San Diego, CA: Plural Publishing, 2020).

4 Lynn Helding, *The Musician's Mind: Teaching, Learning, and Performance in the Age of Brain Science* (Lanham, MD: Rowman & Littlefield Publishing Group, Inc.), 60.

12 Learning, Questioning, and Dealing with Doubt
"Verify It"

As his teaching tenure progressed, Bob found that the students would come to his studio with increasingly solid pedagogical backgrounds. Especially for those he saw as graduate students, they all, on average, displayed a more thorough knowledge of anatomy, physiology, and acoustics than he felt he had at that point in his own education.

He remembers his pedagogy courses during his master's degree at the University of Wisconsin. His professor was Dale Gilbert, who had studied with Andrew B. White at Northwestern University. White's notoriety was partly based on the success of his best-known student, baritone Sherrill Milnes. Bob describes Gilbert as "one of the old guard of voice teachers at the time of Coffin and Vennard." He still remembers the term paper he wrote as part of Gilbert's pedagogy classes. "I can't remember what the topic was," Bob says, "but it came back to me with an A on it, next to which he wrote, 'Obviously you didn't ever have to learn how to sing.'" Bob came up with his own translation of his professor's comment: "Meaning, you don't know shit."

Besides the skills that must be developed during voice lessons, Bob also recognizes the tremendous amount of information that is presented during musical studies—more than any single mind can absorb and retain. He kept this in mind when serving on doctoral committees. Students preparing for their comprehensive exams would often ask him if there were specific subjects or topics he wanted them to prepare. He welcomed such questions, knowing that the field is so vast that no single student could thoroughly prepare for every possible subject. So he did provide certain topics to students as a guide for how to focus their studying. However, he also gave the warning, "You're going to get a damn hard exam." The point was not to see how many facts and how much information students could recall and recite. Instead, he wanted to see how they made connections and how they reasoned their answers when they may not have all the information. "There is a lot that students don't know, and couldn't possibly know, because they're too young to know," he says. "But I always wanted to see how they would stand on their own two feet, and how their minds worked when they didn't know the answers. That's part of academia. You're just not always given the questions before the kid comes in the door with a problem."

Naturally, there is no way for even a long-tenured professor to know everything, either. Therefore, part of what he wanted to see from students when "standing on their own two feet" was a willingness to question the information that was given to them when it did not align with their previous knowledge or experience. He echoed similar sentiments to students throughout his career, as he expressed to me at the outset of our interviews for this book. "As I always said to my students, whether it was in the first song literature class of the year, or even in the studio, 'I want you to doubt everything that I'm telling you. I want you to question and verify that what I'm telling you is the truth. Check,'" he says. "My goal is to tell the truth. So I asked the students to question and doubt everything I told them. Verify it. Don't be afraid to."

When looking back at how much "truth" he feels he received in his own education, he is overwhelmingly complimentary of his past teachers. He knows that, when he was their student, he was young and had limited understanding. He also knows of his propensity for "inactive listening," which he is certain made him a less-than-ideal student to teach.

Considering his voice lessons, in particular, he has difficulty recalling the specific technical elements his teachers addressed, especially in his undergraduate years. The only thing that stands out in his mind was four years of tongue exercises, though he did not know the purpose of those exercises until much later. Once he joined Bjorksten's studio, however, the lessons were more deeply ingrained. Although she had a reputation for being uncompromising, the enduring impression she left on Bob, as stated above, was the importance of being an intelligent musician. "That's probably the most lasting lesson I learned from Bettina: to be smart, to be intelligent, to be able to talk about music, and to be able to lift this information off the page."

Imposter Syndrome

I can relate to Bob's recognition of not always feeling like the easiest student to teach. Hindsight being 20/20, I can see the areas where I was lacking.

Listening back to old cassette recordings of my undergraduate voice lessons is enlightening now that three decades have passed. Hearing them now through "teacher ears," I can tell what results my professors were trying to elicit with their chosen exercises and directions. By the way I responded on the recordings, I can also recognize when I was misunderstanding what was being asked of me. Like Bob, I do not at all blame my teachers for any struggles or failures. In fact, hearing the recordings after this much time has passed, I have tremendous admiration for the tactics they were using. I am now much better able to appreciate the high quality of instruction I was receiving, even though I can tell when a younger me sometimes missed the point.

I have a particular memory from my days as a high school teacher when, in a faculty meeting, one of the administrators was reminding us to be patient with our students. "We have to remember," she said, "that school was pretty easy for us. That's probably a big part of why we became teachers." Although I understood the point she was trying to make, I didn't relate to it at all. School was never easy for me. Just as Bob had doubts about his ability to complete doctoral studies, I had similar qualms when I started at IU. On paper, it probably didn't make sense for either of us to feel that way, but we still did. It's a bit ironic that imposter syndrome is so prevalent among musicians. After all, as performers, we have to appear onstage, act boldly, embrace our vulnerabilities, and sing with confidence. But so many of us admit privately to feeling like we don't belong there or experiencing so much anxiety that it is difficult to perform at our best. The same can apply to our academic work. How can those high-performing actions and low-confidence feelings coexist?

I once interviewed tenor Neil Shicoff for *Classical Singer* on the occasion of his fortieth year as a professional opera singer. He related to me the story of his Metropolitan Opera debut, singing Rinuccio in *Gianni Schicchi*. He says he remembers being in the latter part of the show and mentally reminding himself to keep his breath calm since his aria would be coming up soon. The only problem was he had already sung the aria. "I got good reviews, as I recall, and it was a springboard for me, but I didn't remember it," he says. "It's like when someone's in a car crash and you say, 'What happened?' and they say, 'I don't know.' That's what my debut was like."[1]

I remember in one of my early professional operatic experiences, on a break during a dress rehearsal, one of my castmates asked our music director/conductor if he still gets nervous before performances. He replied, "Before every opening night, I have the same nightmare where someone shows up and exposes me as a fraud. They just pull back the curtain and say, 'See, you don't really belong here.'" This is coming from someone who has conducted multiple shows on Broadway, on national tours, and with major orchestras in the United States and abroad. If he actually was a fraud, it seems likely someone would have figured it out before he racked up such accomplishments.

In an interview for *60 Minutes*, actor Viola Davis (who has achieved EGOT status by winning an Emmy, Grammy, Oscar, and Tony) states that imposter syndrome is something she recognizes in all the artists she has worked with. She acknowledges the armchair psychologizing that leads many people to state that anyone experiencing imposter syndrome simply needs to find more confidence. But she disagrees with that assessment. "It's not about confidence," she says. "It's about that feeling of always feeling you're in process, and that you can be better . . . what it does, on a healthy level, it keeps you humble and it keeps you working."[2]

If the imposter syndrome is most prevalent among performers, I would venture a guess that it is second most prevalent among teachers. Having taught middle school through graduate school, as well as private voice students from ages eight to eighty, I have experienced classes and lessons that made me feel like a knowledgeable, seasoned teacher with much to offer. I have also taught classes and lessons that made me feel like I have no business being in this profession. It brings a particular sort of whiplash when those experiences happen on the same day.

But, if Viola Davis is right, experiencing the inevitable lows that follow the highs simply means that I am still in process as a teacher, that I should stay humble, and that I should keep working. There is a story that professor and speech-language pathologist Kittie Verdolini Abbott often relates in her annual guest lectures at the Summer Vocology Institute. She recalls having a moment of epiphany in her career as a voice therapist that she immediately rushed to share with a colleague. "I just figured out what the point of voice therapy is," she exclaimed. "It's to help the patient get better!" Her colleague, a bit confused, said, "Yes. What did you think the point was?" Verdolini Abbott replied, "Until this moment, I truly thought the purpose of voice therapy was for me to do a good job as clinician."

The goals of wanting the student to improve while also wanting to do a good job as a teacher may go hand in hand. But it likely makes a difference in a voice lesson if I walk into the room focusing more on the second than the first.

Notes

1   Neil Shicoff in Brian Manternach, "Neil Shicoff: A Force for 40 Years," *Classical Singer*, September 2018, 46–7.
2   Viola Davis, "Viola Davis: All Artists Have 'Imposter Syndrome,'" *60 Minutes*, December 6, 2020, YouTube, 3:07, https://www.youtube.com/watch?v=xc3bKzrz4D4.

13 Prioritizing Teaching
Professing Truth

As a teacher, Bob sometimes felt that his experience and expertise were looked down upon due to his lack of professional operatic performance credits. He often felt that the performing he had done (working as a chorister, performing early music, performing faculty recitals) was not as valued as solo operatic credits. "From the very beginning, when I got to Colorado, much of my performance work was dismissed," he says. Although that caused some frustration, and likely some bitterness, it also had another result: "That led me to fight for teaching."

Bob expands on the philosophy behind this choice. "I always believed that a professor is one who professes truth—to teach. That was my title, professor, which implied very strongly that I had to teach," he says. "All I ever wanted to do was to teach. Even in my younger days, I put my all into it. I was constantly working to make my 'professing' better. I loved it. I just wanted people to allow me to do that."

These feelings led to some resentment when he was expected to leave his students in order to go out and perform. "My students were paying for me to be there to teach them," he says. "And yet, administrators were sending me out." He understands the benefit of staying active in the field, as well as the need to build a professional reputation such that students will choose to come and study with him. But once he had established that reputation, as evidenced by a consistently full studio, he felt he should have been released from some of those extra duties. "I not only regretted those absences, but I also resented them," he says. "To be taken away from the very thing I was tasked with doing—teaching—I was resentful of that, the whole time."

Bob recalls how the first time he went up for full professorship, he was denied the promotion. "I was somewhat the cheese that stands alone in this business. Tenure and promotion committees had no idea what the hell to do with me," he says. He did not fit onto the research track, with no peer-reviewed publications to his credit. And he was unwilling to pursue performance opportunities that would take him away from his students. He believes these two factors, particularly the lack of performance credits on his resume, kept him from that advancement in rank when he first applied. It was only later, when colleagues wrote letters of support justifying his focus on teaching instead of performing, that he was finally given the promotion. "The very fact that I had to fill up a proverbial mason jar with beans, so that the counters could see how many beans I had acquired, felt like the behavioral reward system we use with our grandchildren," he says. "If they do something well, they receive a token and they can go to the store and buy something they want. I had to collect beans, too, which I thought was at the expense of teaching."

There is another reason he never truly pursued a performance career more aggressively. He placed a high amount of pressure on himself as a performer. He felt a tremendous responsibility to deliver performances that honored both the composer and poet while also uplifting the audience. "I found performing very uncomfortable," he says. "It wasn't that I was concerned about myself or what people would think of me. But I always wondered if I was doing any decency in lifting the words and music off the printed page and to the ear of the listener. That bothered me to no end. It could create a lot of pre-concert dysentery. I had to give myself a lot of quiet time at home, where there wasn't much conversation. I didn't take those things lightly."

The primary reason, however, was just that he felt so strongly that his job was to teach. "I am not leaving the students for weeks on end," he says. "With the amount of tuition they and their parents are investing? No, I wasn't going to play that game. You could throw me out before I would do that."

Once he got to IU, he regularly invited administrators to come and observe his teaching, so they could fairly judge his efficacy. To his disappointment, no one ever took him up on the offer. "Administrators have an obligation to determine that music is being taught at the very highest degree of truth possible within their institutions," he says. "It's not fair for them to evaluate me or anyone else without coming to see and determine if my teaching has any worth and any substance. They were in control of my salary, but they didn't have all the facts."

His colleagues had better information. It was a couple of years after Bob joined the faculty at IU that accomplished soprano Carol Vaness was hired, as well. Viewed as one of the greatest of her generation, her performance history includes all of the world's major operatic houses alongside a veritable who's who of the most revered singers and conductors of her era. Bob has long admired her as a singer. "I've always regarded Vaness as the great heiress to Maria Callas—even more as I listen to her recordings," he says. "I think there are a lot of parallels there."

This made it all the more meaningful to him when, near the end of his time at IU, Vaness reached out to him. "Out of the blue, I got an email from her that was extremely moving," he says. The email reads: "Did you ever do an opera on stage? Because you are darn good at getting your students to commit to words and music, as opposed to technique. Someone once told me you were a choral man. Is that true? You teach, in my opinion, as if you spent a lifetime on the stage. All of your singers are not just stand-there-and-belt. They are full artists."

He had a similar interaction with cello professor János Starker, the former principal cellist of the Chicago Symphony Orchestra. "We didn't have too many conversations," Bob remembers. "Occasionally we would meet in the hall between lessons or on mailbox trips. When we did talk, it was always about music."

One brief conversation, however, has remained in his memory. Bob always encouraged an open-door policy for his studio, meaning that interested parties were welcome to walk in during lessons and observe his teaching. In fact, he posted a sign on his door stating: "Feel free to enter any and all times." One afternoon early in his first semester of teaching at IU, the door opened and Starker himself entered the studio. Bob recalls, "In his growly Hungarian voice, he said, 'I hear some very good sounds coming out of here.' And he turned to me and said, with rolled r's, 'Are you an opera singer?' I said, 'No, Mr. Starker. I'm just a voice teacher.'" Bob was not at all offended that Starker had assumed he gained his expertise by performing rather than through the academic ranks. "Actually," he says, "I took it as a compliment, for him to wonder how I could get students to sound the way they did without my having performed at the Metropolitan Opera House."

The Performer-Teacher

Of course, having a career as a performer and as a teacher is not necessarily an either/or situation. Every teacher simply has to find the right balance between the demands of these differing responsibilities. One solution for when these teachers are away from campus is for their students to study with other teachers during that time. Another solution is that they receive their lessons in bunches over a period of a few weeks instead of the more traditional model of one lesson per week. There are situations where this can work, especially for graduate-level performers who are working on an abundance of repertoire. But it may present challenges for younger students who are in the earlier stages of developing their technique if there is not sufficient time to practice, explore, and implement vocal instruction between lessons. This was the case with one transfer student I taught who, before coming to our institution, earned a place in the studio of a well-known performer-turned-teacher. Once she got to that campus as a first-year college student, her teacher was on the road so often that she felt she was lacking the consistent guidance she needed to truly develop her technique.

I recall a classmate of mine during graduate school who explained how often his teacher postponed lessons due to his performance schedule and how difficult it could sometimes be simply to get all of his lessons in over the course of a semester. He further explained that, even when the teacher was around, he was often resting his voice while teaching and would refrain from vocal modeling or demonstrations if he had an upcoming engagement. My classmate admitted, "He's just not as good of a teacher when he doesn't demonstrate."

Of course, having a teacher who is an active performer can have other advantages. When these teachers continue to practice, prepare repertoire, and put it on stage, they are engaging in the professional activities their students hope to do. Therefore, they have current experiences that can inform their teaching. They have an insider's view of how the business works and may have connections in the industry to whom they can refer their students when they are ready. And, if students are the same voice type as their teachers, they have a wide body of repertoire they have performed that they may be able to teach to their students with a thorough understanding of the technical approaches needed as well as interpretive advice based on their own performance history of the works.

However, as we must again acknowledge, performing and teaching are different skills. It should not be assumed that someone who is successful as a performer will automatically have similar success as a teacher. To be sure, there are many performer-teachers who have found a workable balance between the two, and many have earned accolades in both arenas. But students on college visits would be wise to inquire as to how often their prospective teachers are away from campus during the school year.

In the end, Bob never wanted to be the kind of teacher who was on the road more often than he was at home. I feel the same way, perhaps in part because that is what was modeled for me by both my teachers and my parents.

My parents were homebodies, to be sure. They were involved in our community, and they had occasional date nights when they would leave my siblings and me with a sitter. But they were home the vast majority of the time they were not at work. This gave them the freedom to attend nearly all the events their four children were involved in (games, concerts, competitions, recitals, etc.). I feel lucky that they gave us quality time as well as a quantity of time. We never had to wonder if they would be there for us.

Several years ago, I took the "love languages" test based on Gary Chapman's 1992 book *The Five Love Languages: How to Express Heartfelt Commitment to Your Mate*.[1] It was no surprise to me when "quality time" ranked as one of my highest love languages. This means that one of the primary ways I express love toward others is to spend time with them, as opposed to other ways, such as giving gifts. This can lead to potential problems if I am giving my time too freely or if I feel it is being taken advantage of. It can also be difficult to find work/life balance if I am too available for students and clients, answering texts or emails during times when my attention is needed elsewhere. Obviously, boundaries must be established and limits must be enforced. But, I recognize that I have been conditioned to give my time abundantly, in no small part because it has always been given so freely to me by my parents and other loved ones, including my teachers.

Note

1 Gary Chapman, *The Five Love Languages: How to Express Heartfelt Commitment to Your Mate* (Chicago, Ill: Northfield Publishing, 1992).

14 What Makes a Good Student? What Makes a Good Teacher?

Often before our Zoom interviews for this book, I would send Bob a list of questions I was interested in exploring. Once he had gathered his thoughts on the subjects, we would schedule our next meetings. One question in particular caught him a bit off guard. "Among the inquiries you shared with me the other day, one question really stopped me dead in my tracks," he says. The question: What makes a good student? "It's such an obvious question," he says. "If I were still teaching, it'd be a question I'd use on a doctoral oral exam, because that's an important issue. And, I must say, I haven't thought about that. Wow."

In forming his answer, he recalls the many meetings he had with prospective students. In these conversations, he would often start with a specific question of his own: Where do you want to be in ten or fifteen years? "Invariably, they would say, and with excitement, 'I want to be at the Met!' Okay. Then the next question was always, 'What's the first thing you want to do when you get up in the morning?' If they didn't say 'sing,' I would tell them their chances of getting to the Met are practically nil."

He remembers that in his own years of development, singing was quite literally the first thing he would do each morning. "This would probably declare me, by others, as being weird," he says. Even so, he has fond memories from his young childhood of closing the door to his bedroom, firing up his portable Victrola record player, and imitating the singers he heard on the recordings. "I did it for hours," he says. "I can't imagine what my father thought of that. It probably disturbed him beyond all. But he would never say it. My mother tolerated it, because of her motherliness, I suppose. Her child was always perfect, no matter how weird he might act. So she never discouraged it. But I knew that I didn't want my bedroom door open during those times. That was a private moment. And I didn't want anybody remarking about it. Even if it were a positive remark."

Perhaps, then, being a bit odd is a characteristic of being a good student. After all, Bob often sought out students who felt no obligation to conform. "I'm attracted to human beings who are out of the norm, I guess, whatever that means. And that's probably another reason why I was a good music student—I was working with other artists who were also out of the norm, to other people.... So, I think a student who wants to get up in the morning and sing—even without an audience, maybe just in the shower, not even in a nice concert hall—that tells me that they may have some interest in this field and may possess the spark of curiosity to learn more about it."

Bob admits that his devotion to music as a practice and as an art, and his expectation that those with professional ambitions should share this devotion, caused some friction in his interpersonal relationships with students and colleagues, and especially with administrators. "As you probably saw from time to time, even at IU, I could be impatient with individuals who didn't look at music as seriously as I did, who didn't have the respect for it. When I detect that, it just drives me up the wall with anger. And I'll fight it. I can't respect any administrators who put other concerns before music, and at a music school, no less. No, music is first. That understanding, I think, is a requirement of being a good student."

Despite these beliefs, Bob never pursued work in upper-level administration, knowing he belonged in the voice studio. He freely admits that he would have made a lousy dean. Instead, he spent a fair amount of time trying to convince those in charge that the way to increase institutional revenue was not through endless fundraising but through the best teaching. "If you give the students the finest teaching, they will come," he says. This mindset influenced his actions on university committees, where he fulfilled the "service" requirement of his contract. "Whether right or wrong, my vote was always on the side of what is best for the students. I am here to serve the students, by challenging them, by instructing them, and by sharing tools that will make their lives easier as performers."

For Bob, the tremendous reverence he extends to music and the teaching of music inspires great humility when he approaches this *holde Kunst*. "I constantly have to work, unfortunately, to extend humility to human beings. I'm not very good at that," he says. "There's a bit of self-absorption that I constantly have to work against, I suppose. But that's all right. As we're instructed, the good Lord loves us and protects and guides us and forgives us and gives us chance after chance after chance. I believe that very strongly. But when it comes to music, I don't play around. Don't abuse it. Don't disrespect it."

Bob closed his thoughts on the subject saying, "This question—what makes a good student—you stopped me in my tracks. I was actually displeased with myself that I hadn't thought of this as much as I should have. So, thank you for a 'Wow' moment."

What Makes a Good Teacher?

I asked Bob this particular question because I suspect there are some positive qualities that all students must possess to learn effectively: motivation, curiosity, and a willingness to make mistakes are a few that come to mind. The obvious related question is, "What makes a good teacher?" Allowing that studio teaching is a two-way street, the burden of responsibility is not entirely on the shoulders of either party. Both contribute to making the situation a success. However, as the one accepting payment for services rendered, the greater onus to deliver is decidedly on the teacher. Perhaps, then, one characteristic of a good teacher is to constantly evaluate whether or not students are getting what they need. This requires ongoing observation, evaluation, and education.

Many of Bob's practices in the voice studio are widely applicable. I know this because I have seen how successful they can be with my own students. Some practices, however, are more circumstantial, representing an effective choice in a specific situation. Perhaps another characteristic of a good teacher is knowing when tried-and-true tactics may apply and when a more inventive, individualized approach is needed.

Considering the two-way street, I acknowledge that what made my studio experience with Bob a success (if I may call it that) was due to what I brought to the studio as much as it was what Bob brought. I don't think that's arrogant to say. It just acknowledges my investment in making the partnership work. I feel the same is true with the students I teach. Maybe another characteristic of a good teacher is to be as invested in students' success as they are.

It's also important to recognize how our collective approach to studio teaching has been shifting in recent years. As Lynn Helding reminds us, "pedagogy is concerned not only with what teachers know, but how students learn."[1] Her work in applying the principles of motor-learning theory to voice training reflects her staunch advocacy of cognitive science as the third pillar of voice pedagogy (alongside voice physiology and voice acoustics). Therefore, it is not enough for teachers to understand the science, art, and craft of singing. We also have to know how it is that students best acquire knowledge and build skills.

As the amount of information—and access to that information—has exponentially increased over the last few decades, teachers now have endless opportunities for continual education. Pioneering voice pedagogue and author Richard Miller (1926–2009) wrote of teachers: "We owe it to our students to be able to take advantage not only of everything that was known 200 years ago, but also of everything that is known today," a philosophy that Helding has since dubbed "The Doctrine of Accumulation."[2] What was already an overwhelming task when Miller's words were published in 1991 has become even more impossible as the ever-growing body of voice-related information has since expanded.

As an example, new teaching approaches that have been promoted in just the last decade include Evidence-Based Voice Pedagogy,[3] the Comprehensive Voice Pedagogy Framework,[4] Fact-Based Voice Pedagogy,[5] and Science-Informed Voice Pedagogy.[6] As we continue to recognize the limitations of traditional models and methodologies and acknowledge the populations they do not adequately serve, there are calls for studio teaching to be more consent-based,[7] trauma-informed,[8] size-inclusive,[9] gender-affirming,[10] neurodiversity-affirming,[11] and student-centered.[12] There are similar calls to move away from teacher-centered environments that reinforce hierarchical power dynamics, like the master-apprentice approach.[13]

There is much to be gained from exploring all the exciting directions in which the field is moving. Not only do these approaches stand to make modern teaching more effective, but they will also make it more inclusive, equitable, and compassionate. Therefore, even if we can never reach Richard Miller's unattainable ideal, we do have a responsibility to learn all we can in the interest of better serving our students.

What makes a good student? What makes a good teacher? Was I a good student? Was Bob a good teacher? Am I a better teacher now than I would have been had I not been Bob's student? (Figure 14.1) I have dedicated a fair amount of time to pondering these questions, unanswerable though they

Figure 14.1 Brian in his voice studio with students Carmin Fisk and Savanna Joy; Brandon Cruz Photography. Courtesy of the University of Utah College of Fine Arts, 2024.

may be. In the last section of this book, I will examine how it is we might evaluate past pedagogues and how we can carry their legacy forward while still honoring the new and necessary directions in which the field is moving.

Notes

1. David Meyer and Lynn Helding, "Practical Science in the Studio: 'No-Tech' Strategies," *Journal of Singing* 77, no. 3 (January/February 2021): 360.
2. Richard Miller, "The Singing Teacher in the Age of Voice Science," in *Vocal Health and Pedagogy*, 3rd ed., ed. Robert Sataloff (San Diego, CA: Plural Publishing, Inc., 1991), 7–10; Lynn Helding, *The Musician's Mind: Teaching, Learning, and Performance in the Age of Brain Science* (Lanham, MD: Rowman & Littlefield Publishing Group, Inc.), x.
3. Kari Ragan, "Defining Evidence-Based Voice Pedagogy: A New Framework," *Journal of Singing* 75, no. 2 (November/December 2018): 157–60.
4. Amelia Rollings Bigler, Katherine Osborne, Chadley Ballantyne, Brian Horne, Kimberly James, Brian Manternach, Yvonne Redman, and Melissa Treinkman, "Voice Pedagogy for the 21st Century: The Summation of Two Summits," *Journal of Singing* 78, no. 1 (September/October 2021): 11–28.

5 American Academy of Teachers of Singing, "In Support of Fact-Based Voice Pedagogy and Terminology," *Journal of Singing* 71, no. 1 (September/October 2014): 9–14.

6 National Association of Teachers of Singing, "Science-Informed Voice Pedagogy Resources," https://www.nats.org/cgi/page.cgi/Science-Informed_Voice_Pedagogy_Resources.html (accessed April 30, 2024).

7 Brian Manternach and David Eggers, "Using Theatrical Intimacy Practices to Create Vocal Health Boundaries," *Journal of Singing* 79, no. 1 (September/October 2022): 73–7, https://doi.org/10.53830/TUBI6925.

8 Elisa Monti, Megan Durham, and Allison Reynolds, "Focusing the Scope: The Voice Practitioner's Role in Trauma-Informed Care," *Journal of Singing* 80, no. 4 (March/April 2024): 455–62, https://doi.org/10.53830/sing.00029.

9 Elizabeth Ann Benson and Kate Rosen, "Anti-Fat Bias in the Singing Voice Studio, Part Two: How to Make a Size Inclusive Voice Studio," *Journal of Singing* 79, no. 5 (May/June 2023): 653–60, https://doi.org/10.53830/KNDP8249.

10 The Voice Lab, "Gender-Affirming Speech and Singing at the Voice Lab," https://thevoicelabinc.thinkific.com/courses/gender-affirming-voice-and-speech-spring-2024 (accessed April 30, 2024).

11 Shannon Coates, "Neurodiversity in the Voice Studio, Clinic, and Performance Space: Using a Neurodiversity Affirming Lens to Build More Inclusive Spaces for Singers, Part 1, Current Understanding of Neurodiversity," *Journal of Singing* 79, no. 2 (November/December 2022): 213–19, https://doi.org/10.53830/VHSX6387.

12 Travis Sherwood, "Evolving the Master-Apprentice Tradition: A Pathway Back to a Student-Centered Pedagogy," *Journal of Singing* 80, no. 1 (September/October 2023): 13–22, https://doi.org/10.53830/GTOJ3285.

13 Ibid.; Brian Manternach, "Master of None: Challenging the Master-Apprentice Model," *Journal of Singing* 80, no. 4 (March/April 2024): 447–54, https://doi.org/10.53830/sing.00028.

Part III
Legacy

Legacy

15 On the Shoulders of Giants
Assessing, Evaluating, and Citing

At the end of every semester, college and university students are asked to complete surveys providing feedback on the effectiveness of their courses and their instructors. I know teachers who welcome this feedback, seeing it as an opportunity to adjust their approaches and improve their practices. I know others who dismiss it, believing, I suppose, that the students don't know what they don't know and, thus, can't fairly evaluate the instruction they're receiving. One noteworthy evaluation Bob remembers from early in his Colorado tenure was from a student who wrote, with likely unintended irony, "Professor Harrison often repeats himself; he is overly repetitive."

Naturally, there are many factors that can impact the usefulness of this feedback. For instance, how pertinent are the questions to the course? How many of the students enrolled in the course actually complete the surveys? If the surveys are voluntary, do the comments represent the extremes of experiences (the lovers and the haters), or do they represent the experiences of the majority of the class? Regardless, each semester, college and university teachers are offered at least one student-led evaluation of their performance.

Is there anything to be gained by undertaking a similar evaluation of Bob's teaching now that he is well into retirement? More broadly, is it worth taking the time to evaluate any teachers and practices from previous generations? Time moves on and so do the fields of vocal performance and voice pedagogy. What is the benefit of looking back?

An apt justification is provided by Stephen F. Austin, former professor of voice and vocal pedagogy at the University of North Texas. From 2005 to 2016, Austin wrote fifty-nine articles for the "Provenance" column of the *Journal of Singing*, which were later compiled into a book of the same name. The goal of his writing was to present historical voice pedagogy texts and treatises, view them through a "contemporary lens," and place them into a modern context. In the introduction to his book, Austin writes,

> *I have often commented that voice teachers are among the few professionals who can practice without a thorough knowledge of the history of their craft.... However, I believe that there is much to be gained from looking to our past. It is said that any culture that does not appreciate its own history is doomed to failure. Important lessons may be learned from those who have gone before us, things to remember to do and things that shouldn't be done.... Truth doesn't change over time. Neither do effective teaching methods. Even as styles have changed, the voice functions as it always has. Methods and ideas that were developed out of successful experience in any age have something to say to us today.[1]*

Bob spoke often in our conversations of his desire to present the truth to his students, as best he understood it. Austin believes that neither truth nor effective teaching methods change over time. Therefore, it seems the best we stand to gain from revisiting past teachers and their practices is a bit of truth. This may come in the form of "things to remember to do" or "things that shouldn't be done." It may also remind us of things we once knew that we have since forgotten. And it may cause us to take a hard look at whether or not newer practices are any more effective than historical ones. As the sayings go, if "everything old is new again," we need not "reinvent the wheel."

Citing Your Sources

A second question to consider is how often in voice lessons we should acknowledge to our students where our ideas and practices come from. Is it enough to just focus on the ideas or do we have to cite the sources? After all, when I visit my doctor, I don't ask who invented the medications I may be prescribed. I just want help addressing whatever malady I may be experiencing. When I buy a new cell phone, I'm interested to know what new capabilities it has, but I never ask who developed the technology that allowed for these added bells and whistles. Does it matter if I cite where all the ideas, philosophies, and practices come from that I use in my teaching?

Additionally, when it comes to certain practices that are ubiquitous in voice instruction, is it enough to mention where I learned a concept or do I have to research who the first person was to present it? As an example, singing teachers have been incorporating nasal consonants and lip trills into vocalizes long before anyone knew the phrase "semi-occluded vocal tract exercises." When we use these vocalizes, should we cite the early pedagogues who used them, or should we credit the voice scientists who were the first to provide an in-depth explanation of what these exercises accomplish? Or, can we simply use the exercises without pausing to cite the sources?

Similarly, what is the protocol for using more specific ideas? If I use the phrase "No Parking" or "No air, no sound, no dollars," do I need to explain that I learned those phrases (and the concepts behind them) from Bob? Is it a disservice to him to allow students to assume that they are my ideas?

I can offer two parts to this answer. First, we are all "standing on the shoulders of giants." I would venture to say that none of us who have achieved any degree of success in our field have done so without a tremendous amount of help. The many theories, philosophies, and exercises our predecessors have left for us mean that we don't have to start from square one every time we step into the voice studio. Therefore, at the very least, it is gracious to acknowledge those whose work has made us more effective teachers. And it's probably fair to say that the world would stand to benefit from an overall increase in graciousness.

Second, when it comes to written work and formal presentations, academic honesty actually *requires* that we provide citations identifying where we came across our ideas. Indeed, the format of most research papers includes a "review of literature" section, which essentially shows readers what work has already been done in an area that led authors to the point where their research could begin. The same is true of academic presentations. Scholars owe it to their audiences to demonstrate how their work was influenced by others, lest they leave the impression that it is based entirely on their own original thought. This is so important that some people found to have violated these practices have been fired from academic positions or have had their degrees revoked.

But, when it comes to working in the studio, do we have the same responsibility to cite our sources? Do we have to pause in every voice lesson to say, "I learned this exercise from X," or "Here's something I saw Y do in a workshop," or even "Let's try this thing I just read about in Z"? The answer here is less clear. I doubt anyone has ever been fired for providing inadequate citations during a voice lesson. That being said, I believe there are a few reasons it may be useful to occasionally explain to students how we came upon our current practices.

First, for curious students, it may lead them to other sources where they can find further inspiration. When an exercise or a concept seems particularly effective, sharing where we learned that information may open up an area of exploration that can lead them to additional meaningful discoveries.

Second, it demonstrates that, as teachers, we are students ourselves who are constantly learning from others. It eschews the master-apprentice approach where students come to our studios to be given answers from all-knowing teachers. Instead, we reveal ourselves as co-investigators with our students, using all the tools we have available to us in order to achieve desired results. If we never cite our sources, it may lead students to believe that every idea, concept, and practice we use is entirely our own, which is both false and dishonest—a sin of omission. To paraphrase the musical *The Robber Bridegroom*, steal with style, but cite your sources.

Third, as stated above, it's simply a gracious act. Acknowledging those who have offered something positive to our teaching demonstrates a generosity of spirit and a kindness that only stands to contribute to an environment rife for learning.

Of course, I would not expect that ideas would be cited in voice lessons as precisely as Bob quoted Shirlee Emmons ("I want the Coffin exercise on page 85 of the red book."). And, to be sure, it can interrupt the flow of lessons to constantly interject with lengthy explanations of how we came to learn individual practices. But I also know that when my students respond positively to a concept, I appreciate being able to share articles, books, videos, or other sources that may further benefit their education.

In my own studio, when discussions of efficient breathing for singing come up, I nearly always cite Bob and his idea of breathing with an intention to communicate. I remind my students, as he reminded me, that the inhalation is part of the communicative process and that clear intent tends to lead to efficient function.

When my students become a bit too cavalier in changing notes and rhythms in ways that seem to serve their egos more than the message of the music, Bob creeps into my studio, as well. I take on my best imitation of his tone and inflection and say, "As my teacher once told me, 'You need to go write your own damn song! Stop recomposing this one!'" I accompany these words with my best facial expression of mock disgust that I was on the receiving end of more times than I can count. I know my intention has landed when I receive the same smile or eye roll from my students that I'm sure I gave Bob in those moments.

When my students are discouraged, usually after a failed audition or a clouded vision of how they can make a place for themselves in the industry, I draw once again upon Bob's example. At IU, after I had received some dispiriting comments in a master class performance with a world-renowned singer as to what she felt were the dim prospects I had for success, Bob shared with me some of the negative comments he had received throughout his career. He reminded me that this is a subjective business and reaffirmed his belief in my potential. Relating this story seems to provide perspective to my students that they can tap into whenever inevitable disappointments arise.

In each of these instances, I feel the point is made more effectively when I specifically cite Bob. Demonstrating that the lessons my students are learning are the same ones that I had to learn, and by pinpointing when and how it was that I learned them, emphasizes that they are not alone in their journey. Although their paths are uniquely their own, the experiences of their teacher (and their teacher's teacher) may provide useful direction.

Note

1 Stephen F. Austin, *Provenance: Historic Voice Pedagogy Viewed through a Contemporary Lens* (Gahanna, OH: Inside View Press, 2017), viii–ix.

16 How to Fairly Evaluate
Contextualizing a Career

If we do believe that there is usefulness in evaluating teachers who have completed their careers, the next question is *how* we might assess them. What is the most meaningful way to measure their effectiveness? How can we contextualize their work to fairly gauge its impact?

In the grand scheme of things, Bob has not been retired for all that long (less than a decade, as of this writing). But, when we look at the arc of his entire career, he taught for more years in the previous century than he did in the current one. He earned his first full-time teaching position in 1978. He finished his terminal degree in 1986, thirty years before he retired from teaching in 2016. Certain events that had significant impacts on voice education occurred after he had completed his career. He did not teach through the Covid-19 pandemic, so he was never asked to shift a full-time studio to an online platform. He retired before the "Me Too" movement led to the firing of several prominent musicians and before the Black Lives Matter movement caused all arts organizations and educational institutions to take a hard look at their complicity in systems of exclusion.

I started studying with Bob less than three years after the tragedies of 9/11. The devastation of Hurricane Katrina occurred while I was his student. Most college students today (and even many graduate students) were either not yet alive during those events or are too young to have memories of them.

We are all products of our eras. Just as we discuss how best to evaluate teachers of his generation, my peers and I will be similarly evaluated by those of later generations. Will they feel that we kept valued traditions alive while still adjusting to the needs of modern times? Which opportunities for change will they feel we either collectively ignored or insufficiently addressed? In the final evaluation, I suspect none of us will come out with a perfect record.

All of this evaluating has to occur with an awareness of what tools were available at the time and how widespread they were. I remember my sister discussing how to handle "screen time" with her children while they were growing up in the 2010s. At the time, she fielded comments from parents of earlier generations who made unhelpful comments like, "My kids didn't have cell phones or iPads and they turned out fine," to which she sometimes responded, "Well, congratulations on keeping your kids away from technology that didn't exist yet."

With that in mind, we have to consider to what degree Bob and the teachers of his era had access to certain information. As I mentioned, many of the teaching approaches promoted today either did not exist or were not widely known during Bob's career. If his teaching was, for instance, consent-based or student-centered, it was not because he had access to the frameworks as they have been spelled out in recent years.

To single out one of these approaches, the term "Science-Informed Voice Pedagogy" was not discussed in print until May 2020, to my knowledge.[1] The NATS Science-Informed Voice Pedagogy Institute had its inaugural iteration in the summer of 2023.[2] Voice science has certainly influenced studio voice teaching during my lifetime in ways that may not have been anticipated in Bob's early career. Even so, some of what we know now was available back then, even if it was more difficult to come by. The revised and "greatly enlarged" edition of William Vennard's seminal text, *Singing: The Mechanism and the Technic*, was published in 1967, the year Bob graduated from high school. Richard Miller's *The Structure of Singing: System and Art in Vocal Technique* was published in 1986, the year Bob finished his doctorate. Both books intentionally incorporated voice science in ways that had not been similarly done in pedagogy texts up to that point. Both were widely known and available for the majority of Bob's career. He also had the advantage of working at the University of Colorado, following in the pedagogical footsteps of Berton Coffin and Barbara Doscher. Though Coffin retired from CU in 1977 (four years before Bob was hired), his books were also widely available and his influence undoubtedly lived on through Doscher, his former student. In fact, Doscher offers Coffin her "heartfelt love and gratitude" in the preface of her own vocal pedagogy textbook, *The Functional Unity of the Singing Voice*.[3] Doscher's book is also considered influential enough that it was recently posthumously re-released with added commentary from Doscher's former students and colleagues (including a section written by Bob). So, he did not exactly teach from a pedagogical desert island.

The way that elements of voice science are applied to the voice studio has continued to develop and has been made even more accessible in the twenty-first century. For instance, tools like spectrograms have dramatically improved in quality and accessibility. When I was a student at IU, the VoceVista software was still in its early stages. Today, spectrograms of remarkably high quality can be downloaded to smartphones for free.

There are still some holdouts who question whether or not voice science has actually benefited voice teaching. They remind us that the great singers of previous generations made their mark without the benefit of much of the technology and functional understanding that exists today. Undoubtedly, great singing has been occurring for centuries, even among some singers who had little or no formal training. Therefore, to say that present-day technologies and understandings are absoutely necessary in order for effective, communicative, functionally efficient singing to occur is patently false. As a demonstration, Bob recalls a story of a conversation between previous IU faculty members. As it was told to him, Ralph Appleman—voice pedagogue and author of *The Science of Vocal Pedagogy: Theory and Application*—was always after his colleague, internationally acclaimed soprano Eileen Farrell, to sing into a spectrograph so he could analyze her sound. "She would have nothing to do with it," Bob says. "Following a number of requests to do so and to get him off her back, as it were, she gave in to his request, and entered a sample into the spectrograph. Appleman's reply was, 'Look Eileen, your singing is off the resonance.' To which Farrell replied, 'Well, Ralph, no one ever said that to me before. I guess I should give all that money back!'"

However, we should seek to use whatever tools we have at our disposal. I have never felt hindered by having more information—in the voice studio or in any other situation. Effective voice teaching requires advanced listening skills, intuitive application, and some degree of trial and error—simply understanding voice science will never be enough. And there is not, nor will there likely ever be, a foolproof checklist or methodology that will lead to desired results 100 percent of the time. Even so, voice science can be an important partner as we continue to look for ways to bring efficiency and expressivity into our teaching, even if we don't share all of the minutiae of what we know with our students.

After my time at IU, as I continued to pursue studies in voice science (and I have so much more to learn), the more I started to realize how much voice science Bob already knew back when I was his student. At least, much of his teaching seemed to reflect a deeper knowledge in that area than I was ever aware he possessed. Even more remarkable, he applied that understanding to studio instruction in practical ways without bogging students down with information that was unnecessary at the moment.

As noted earlier, Bob believes that many teachers in the current era have become quite adept at developing functionally efficient "singing machines." I suspect that much of this could be due to modern applications of voice science, which may allow for quicker, more accurate assessments of functional inefficiencies. However, Bob does question whether that focus within studio instruction has led to singing that is more expressive and more communicative. As he states, "I think these tools of voice science are absolutely outstanding. But they should never be the end-all. If what we do is merely a science, and the outcome is to get good computer readings on the sound of somebody's voice, we will not be serving the deemed and deserved great composers. Their work is for naught. We have to take the known science of the time and use it to get to the goal of communicative singing, which as I stated previously can be taught."

Therefore, if we are to consider to what degree Bob made use of the information available to him as part of our rubric of evaluation, he was years ahead of his time when it comes to the incorporation of voice science. Still, he never allowed that knowledge to supersede the goal of serving music, serving composers, and serving audiences.

Notes

1 Lynn Helding, "Science-Informed Vocal Pedagogy: Motor Learning, Deliberate Practice and the Challenge of Cognitive Dissonance," in *The Routledge Companion to Interdisciplinary Studies in Singing, Volume II: Education*, ed. Gudmundsdottir, Beynon, Ludke, Cohen (Abingdon: Routledge Publishing, May 2020), 182–93.

2 National Association of Teachers of Singing, "NATS Science-Informed Voice Pedagogy Institute," https://www.nats.org/Science-Informed_Pedagogy_Institute.html (accessed May 1, 2024).

3 Barbara M. Doscher, *The Functional Unity of the Singing Voice, 2nd Edition Expanded with an Introduction by John Nix* (Lanham, MD: Rowman & Littlefield Publishing Group, Inc.), xii.

17 **Judicious Emulation**
When to Turn Away from What We Were Taught

I would argue that another criterion for evaluation is how teachers deviate from the ways they were taught. As Austin states, there are "things to remember to do and things that shouldn't be done" when looking back at our teachers and their practices. Bob and I agree that students should not become facsimiles of their teachers, defaulting to the same methods simply because they are known. It sometimes takes thoughtfulness and conscious effort to adopt philosophies that run counter to those of our teachers.

This may be particularly difficult in the field of classical music, which places a high value on tradition. As much as modern opera companies work to innovate, commission new works, and seek to foster continued development of the genre, most of these same companies draw their biggest audiences when they program the same handful of tried-and-true operas that have been performed for centuries.

Voice teaching also draws heavily upon traditional methods. Some practices used in the voice studio seem to carry additional credibility if they have been passed down from teacher to teacher. Naturally, we need not abandon practices that are clearly effective. On the other hand, just because an exercise dates back to Manuel Garcia II does not mean that it will be the right choice for every student.

Bob refers to Bettina Bjorksten—his voice teacher at the University of Wisconsin-Madison—as his greatest influence, attributing many of the most valuable lessons he learned to her. He further credits her with recognizing potential in him as a teacher that he had not yet seen in himself. He always appreciated the way she treated him like a colleague rather than a student, which was not typical for her. "She never came down on me," he says, "though she certainly could have, given her reputation as an old-school, hard-nosed teacher."

I didn't specifically ask Bob how his teaching may have deviated from Bjorksten's. Even so, one aspect of her instruction came up in our conversations that he intentionally chose not to adopt. "The undergraduate students she had—she was ruthless with them," he says. He remembers a specific instance when a young, talented undergraduate student came in to sing for Bjorksten's weekly master class. After the student sang, Bjorksten said, with the thick German accent she maintained throughout her life, "Now, can you give me some idea, my dear, what the text is about?" The question was followed by a long silence while the singer tried to come up with an appropriate response. Although it was clear to everyone that the student did not know the answer, Bjorksten allowed the silence to continue for even longer before very quietly saying, "I have all the time in the world for your answer. We all shall wait." After an interminable, uncomfortable silence felt by everyone in the studio, the young singer broke into tears. Bjorksten responded, "I guess you have provided your only answer. You may leave the stage."

I have heard many teachers retell similar stories from their education and, as a student, I have experienced some of my own firsthand. I have even heard from some teachers who seem to pride themselves on the "tough love" approach they take in their studios. A few have shared examples with me, delivered with unchecked glee, that the students seemingly got what they deserved for being unprepared. Bob took no joy in retelling this memory from Bjorksten's studio, admitting, "I never felt that I could go that far as a teacher." As the saying goes, those who claim to be brutally honest often seem to be more interested in the brutality than the honesty.

By no means did Bob shy away from difficult conversations or sternness in the studio when he felt it was warranted. He especially had little patience for students who would come in with what he perceived to be an attitude of arrogance, believing they were more advanced than their performance indicated. He would sometimes offer these students some perspective. "Occasionally, I had to tell students, 'If you were as good as you think you are, you would not have to come into the studio each and every week to work with me. But, by the very fact that you have to keep coming in here, you may not be as good as that.'" Even so, he had his limits. "I was never like [former men's basketball coach] Bobby Knight was at IU, throwing chairs," he says. A low bar, to be sure. But the classical music industry is still infuriatingly slow to oust those who throw their own proverbial chairs at the very people they are charged with instructing and inspiring.

Contrary to some of the conservatory professors I have sung for in the past, who exuded an attitude of, "Prove to me that you're worth my time," Bob was especially intentional about creating a comfortable studio environment when a student was working with him for the first time. His main priority was to validate what they were doing and to honor the work they had done thus far. At initial lessons, or in trial lessons with students auditioning for his studio, he always wanted them to feel as though they were putting their best foot forward. "I have said to students, when they're auditioning to come into the studio, 'Please sing for me something where you can give your best performance,'" he says. "'What do you enjoy singing? Where might I see and hear your personality shine? Where are you the most comfortable? Give me that piece.'"

It's significant that his first requests were to see what sort of music students enjoy singing and where they feel their personalities come through most clearly in their performances. This is in contrast to asking them to make their most impressive sounds, show off their highest notes, or display their most virtuosic singing. He understands that when we sing where we are most technically comfortable, we are allowed to be the most authentic in our expression. Still today, when choosing repertoire for auditions or vocal competitions, many singers bring in the most technically challenging pieces in their active repertoire. While this may allow for some impressive vocal acrobatics, it often comes at the expense of expression and artistry, which Bob forever prioritizes.

It's also significant that Bob welcomed students to choose their own repertoire rather than providing a list of their prepared rep from which he would select what they would sing. Whether he knew it or not, allowing students this sort of agency in something as basic as repertoire choice is a significant part of the student-centered approach. This is another important element of his teaching upon which we can evaluate his impact favorably, a practice which—according to my experience—was not widely practiced at the time.

18 Conclusion
My Teacher's Student

It's natural to wonder at times how we might be remembered when our working days are complete. To ponder our "legacy" seems to elevate or add weight to the exercise. In various dictionaries, the first definition of legacy usually refers to money or property left to someone in a last will and testament. I find that disappointing, as though our primary significance in the world is related to the money, possessions, or "stuff" we leave behind. Certainly, financial legacies can have a profound impact, providing opportunities for those with fewer means. Indeed, the survival of many arts organizations and educational institutions is dependent on donations from those who have the funds to give and an interest in the cause to which they are giving. But most of us will never have the sort of wealth that leads to seeing our names on the front of buildings, so there must be other consequential metrics to consider.

Of course, when possessions are passed on to us by loved ones, they can be incredibly meaningful. In the end, however, those objects are only symbols—reminders of personal interactions, time spent, and experiences shared. Physical possessions will eventually degrade with time, but the true value of what they represent endures. This is reflected in the second listed definition of legacy, which describes the long-lasting impact of events, actions, or a person's life. Rather than our wealth or our possessions, our legacies as teachers will be based on our words and actions and how they impacted our students.

Just as I believe that the term "artist" is one that should be assigned by audiences rather than claimed by individuals, our legacies will also ultimately be defined by others. There is a reason that award nominations, retirement tributes, and even obituaries are usually composed by someone other than the individual being honored, recognized, or remembered. They aren't meant to be autobiographical. These reflections on a person's life and work are purposely provided by outside observers, which likely makes them more accurate.

If I were to truly define Bob's legacy, I would have to engage in much more extensive research than I did when preparing this book. I would need the input of a wide range of students and colleagues with whom Bob has worked throughout his career. I would seek their thoughts on his impact and to what degree they still use and pass on his philosophies and practices. That would be a worthy project. As stated earlier, limiting this book to my own experiences essentially provides a case study of one teacher-student relationship. The advantage of this approach is that it can provide a deep dive into our particular dynamic, thoroughly examining how he, as a teacher, has influenced me, his student. The disadvantage is that my feelings and conclusions, as reflected here, may not be widely shared. Had I studied with Bob longer than I did, this may be a different book. Had I attended CU for my bachelor's or master's degree and studied with Bob at that time, I would likely have had different experiences to report. The same would probably be true if I had a time machine and could go back and work with Bob in his early years of teaching.

It's also entirely possible, given the unique relationship that is formed through the dynamic of individual voice lessons, that some of Bob's students may read this book and find that their experiences do not align with how he is described, outside of the occasional anecdote or oft-repeated phrase. I suppose that is to be expected.

When I was in the middle of my interviews with Bob, I was talking about this book with a colleague who has also dedicated a significant amount of time to preserving the methods and memories of one of his past teachers. We discussed the approach I was planning to take with the book, to show areas of agreement as well as disagreement. He nodded his head, but then he said, "Of course, it's much easier to write these kinds of things about someone after they're dead." That's probably true.

Although I wasn't plagued by constant worry, wondering what Bob would think about my reflections once he saw them in writing, I was certainly conscious of the fact that he would eventually read them, even if that thought lived mostly in the back of my mind. But, I also believe that it would not do justice to Bob's life and career if I only focused on his positive influences. History has been told through a selective lens for too long. The minute we start to idolize anyone, we tend to hide or explain away their imperfections. I wouldn't expect anyone to do that to me, so I will not do it to someone I admire as much as Bob.

That being said, my experiences with Bob, and my memories of those experiences, were and are overwhelmingly positive. As I explained in the introduction, this book contains acknowledged bias since it is written from my perspective alone. However, there is one more element of Bob's teaching worth highlighting that is well-supported in the research literature and not just a reflection of my personal opinions.

There have been a number of published studies that examine how physicians' demeanor can influence how well patients follow through with their directions and advice, whether that be taking prescribed medications, engaging in therapy exercises, or changing elements of their lifestyle. In certain studies, patients who perceived their physicians to be business-like were less satisfied with their doctor-patient interactions and were, therefore, less likely to follow directions from those physicians. Conversely, patients who perceived their doctors to be warm and caring were more likely to stick to the programs and procedures prescribed by those doctors.[1] In short, the doctors who were perceived to be warm and caring were also viewed as competent, while those perceived as being cold and aloof were considered to be incompetent.[2] As Titze and Verdolini Abbott bluntly state in their book *Vocology: The Science and Practice of Voice Habilitation*, "As a clinician, if your patients like you, they are more likely to follow your advice than if they don't like you."[3] These attitudes may extend to those of us in other fields, as well.

Another study, published in 2006 in the *Journal of Singing*, examined the personal interactions of studio teachers and students. Titled "Rapport and Motivation in the Applied Studio," author Jo Clemmons observed the teaching of four master teachers from the NATS Intern Program. She then interviewed the teachers as well as twenty of their students. Among her conclusions, she states, "The analysis of this data suggests that interpersonal relationship is crucial to the success of applied lessons and creates an emotional connection that empowers learning in a dynamic way. Rapport fuels student motivation, and when found in the context of expert teaching, can lead to the empowerment and competency of students."[4]

Like the competent physicians above, Bob was insistently warm and caring in our voice lessons. I was never made to feel that I was merely an instrument being trained for professional-level production. I never felt that I was just a number or that he was clocking his time with me until a more-talented student who was more deserving of his expertise would arrive. I felt supported, both professionally and personally, which allowed me to take the sorts of risks that are necessary for creative expression and meaningful growth. Along the way, I always knew that Bob's interest and investment were in *me* and not just in my voice.

When I was a high school teacher, a principal once said in a faculty meeting, "The most important thing you can do as a teacher is to love your students and to make sure they know it." As the research suggests, such feelings and actions, and the interpersonal connections they help establish, may actually lead to greater student performance and achievement. Unsurprisingly, it seems being a better human also makes one a better teacher.

Though effective pedagogy, I suspect Bob's motivation for operating in this way was taken from another source. As part of the Sermon on the Mount found in the Gospel of Matthew, the "Golden Rule" calls us to "Do unto others as you would have them do unto you." My younger self believed the primary message of the "Do unto others" part was that we should all simply be nice to each other—we should avoid bullying and bad-mouthing and prioritize peace and harmony. From this frame of mind, questions or challenges could be seen as hostile since they may disrupt our pleasant equilibrium. But music that avoids all dissonance risks banality. Teaching that does not challenge risks placating. In his teaching, Bob placed just as much emphasis on the "as you would have them do unto you" part of the Golden Rule. He wanted to be challenged. He expected it. He was as desperate to grow and evolve as he wanted each of his students to be.

For as long as I have known Bob, he has had strong opinions that he is not shy about voicing, as so much of this book demonstrates. As his student, rather than feeling pressure to adopt his ideas, I always felt encouraged and inspired to explore the depths of my own experiences as much as he has his own—to challenge my own convictions, to inform them with the best of what I have learned, and to infuse them with the best of who I am. This lesson, when applied, is just as valuable outside of the voice studio as within it.

A Teacher's Influence

As I was growing up, people often said to me, "You sure are your father's (or mother's) son." It was most often said in relation to a physical feature or personality trait of mine that seems to have originated with one of them. I'd like to think that, most often, the comment was intended as a compliment—an indication that I may have picked up some of the deeper characteristics and ways of being that I admire in my parents. In that way, it recognizes the parts of me that have come from them, even as they manifest themselves in ways that are my own. Whenever someone who doesn't know my parents asks me, "Where did you ever learn to . . . " or "How did you become so . . . " I feel a certain responsibility to acknowledge Mom and Dad as my first teachers and the inspiration for much of my foundational life principles.

On the other hand, sometimes the comment is in regard to some of the less-flattering characteristics I have picked up from my parents, like having too many unfinished projects going on at once or leaving used toothpicks around the house. In those cases, I'm presented with a not-so-subtle opportunity for self-examination. Just because I have learned something from people I love doesn't mean it can't be changed if it doesn't serve me (or those who happen upon the discarded toothpicks).

Curiously, no one has ever said to me, "You sure are your teacher's student." Is that because it's just not a common phrase, or is a teacher's influence not so easily noticeable in their students?

When author Wendell Berry was asked to reflect on the influence of his teacher and mentor, Stanford professor and Pulitzer Prize-winning author Wallace Stegner, he thought back to when he was a student in Stegner's writing seminar in 1958. Berry writes,

> *When I sit at my worktable now I am aware of certain attitudes, hesitations, and insistences that I think are traceable to that seminar thirty-four years ago. I wish I could say that I then understood him as an influence—that I saw what he was about, or saw how to apply his example to my own life. But the fact is that at that time I did not understand him as an influence, and the reason was that at that time I did not know what kind of influence I was going to need. . . . As I failed to understand him as an influence when I first knew him, so have I failed to know very exactly how his influence has grown upon me; it has been involved in my life as I have lived it.[5]*

It could be surmised that when I showed up at IU in 2004, without a private voice teacher, I didn't know what kind of influence I was going to need. But, I suppose, when the student is ready, the teacher will appear. As I have said, education is a two-way street. Had I been able to join either of the studios I had hoped to be part of when I applied to IU, I am certain I would have had a positive experience. But, I am quite happy that things worked out the way they did.

I also relate to Berry's assessment that Stegner's influence has grown upon him and been involved in his life as he has lived it. At some point, our teachers' ideas meld with our own in ways that make it difficult to see the exact moment when the baton was passed along. Recently, I was invited to give a vocal workshop at a high school where one of my former students is a teacher. At the end of the school day, she asked her students, "How many of you learned something new today?" Thankfully, many hands went up. Then she asked, "How many of you saw or heard something that you've seen or heard from me?" Just as many hands went up. Afterward, she said to me, "I forgot all the things I learned from you until I saw you working with my students and realized, 'Oh, I guess that's where I got that.'" It's entirely likely that some of what she learned from me, I had learned from Bob, and he had learned from his teacher Bettina Bjorksten, and she had learned from her teacher Ria Ginster, and she had learned from her teacher Louis Bachner,[6] and on and on it goes.

To be fair, I did pay tuition for the education I received at IU. And Bob was paid a salary for his work, which he felt compelled him to ensure his students were getting the best return on their investment. I paid him for a service that he provided, and I left a satisfied customer. On paper, our transaction was complete the minute I received my diploma. And yet, I believe that the teacher-student dynamic in the voice studio is so much more than transactional—the lessons learned can last well beyond the final voice lesson.

Berry reflects further on Stegner,

> He did not suggest that all our problems were solvable. But there was in his presence and bearing the implication that we could work at our problems, and that we should. I thought, and think still, that he was a good teacher.[7]

Am I my teacher's student? Undoubtedly. Every day that I walk into my own teaching studio, my goal is to do the best I can with all that I have to give, as Bob did. I continue to do so imperfectly. I recognize the many ways I carry Bob's influence into the studio, in ways that are both his and my own. And, like Bob, I feel compelled to keep learning, listen more intently, and try even harder to be the teacher my students deserve as I continue journeying forth in this profession.

No parking allowed.

Notes

1. Barbara M. Korsch, Ethel K. Gozzi, and Vida Francis, "Gaps in Doctor-patient Communication: I. Doctor-patient Interaction and Patient Satisfaction," *Pediatrics* 42, no. 5 (1968): 855–71; Barbara M. Korsch and Vida Francis Negrete, "Doctor-Patient Communication," *Scientific American* 227, no. 2 (1972): 66–75; Vida Francis, Barbara M. Korsch, and Marie J. Morris, "Gaps in Doctor-patient Communication: Patients' Response to Medical Advice," *New England Journal of Medicine* 280, no. 10 (1969): 535–40; as cited in Ingo R. Titze and Katherine Verdolini Abbott, *Vocology: The Science and Practice of Voice Habilitation* (Salt Lake City: National Center for Voice and Speech, 2010), 248.

2. Zeev Ben-Sira, "The Function of the Professional's Affective Behavior in Client Satisfaction: A Revised Approach to Social Interaction Theory," *Journal of Health and Social Behavior* 17 (1976): 3–11; Zeev Ben-Sira, "Affective and Instrumental Components in the Physician-patient Relationship: An Additional Dimension of Interaction Theory," *Journal of Health and Social Behavior* 21 (1980): 170–80; as cited in Titze and Verdolini Abbott, *Vocology*, 248.

3. Titze and Verdolini Abbott, *Vocology*, 248.

4. Jo Clemmons, "Rapport and Motivation in the Applied Studio," *Journal of Singing* 63, no. 2 (November/December 2006): 205.

5. Wendell Berry, "The Momentum of Clarity," in *The Geography of Hope: A Tribute to Wallace Stegner*, ed. Page Stegner and Mary Stegner (San Francisco, CA: Sierra Club Books, 1996), 72.

6. Author of *Dynamic Singing: A New Approach to Free Voice Production* (New York, NY: A. A. Wyn, Inc., 1944).

7. Berry, "The Momentum of Clarity."

Appendix I
Nacht und Träume

To give an example of how Bob interprets music, and to give some insight into how he approaches a song and what details he is drawn to, he suggested we work through a piece of music together. The piece he selected is Nacht und Träume, *a poem by Matthäus von Collin that was set by Franz Schubert. The score he used for the analysis, which was edited by Eusebius Mandyczewski (1875–1929), is in the public domain and available at https://imslp.org/wiki/Nacht_und_Tr%C3%A4ume,_D.827_(Schubert,_Franz).*[1] *Bob's intention was not to do a thorough, measure-by-measure analysis. Rather, it was to indicate the sorts of details that caught his attention and drew his curiosity, with the hope that readers may consider some of the same questions in the music they are preparing to perform.*

A secondary intent of this appendix is to provide a relatively unedited window into how our twenty hours of interviews went. I have preserved the conversation below as it occurred, with sidebars and tangents intact. Therefore, the words below are entirely Bob's with only light edits and some of my editorial interjections in brackets (Figure A.1).

At some point in time, I read a quote—I believe it was by [Arnold] Schoenberg—stating that we must understand when we pick up a piece of music that we have a record of a composer's inner thoughts. I can't tell you how many times I have heard people say, "I wish we had a recording of Schubert at the piano. Then we'd have an understanding of what Schubert was thinking." To which I would say, "What's wrong with this record [the score]?" We've got an awful lot of Schubert's thoughts right here. You can bitch and moan all you want that you don't have a record of Schubert at the piano with a singer with whom he worked. Well, we don't have that. Get over it. But we do have a record of his thoughts right here in the music.

The first thing we have a responsibility to do—because these are the thoughts of a very accomplished man—is to make sure that they're accurate. So, fortunately, musicologists have created Urtext editions, which we can get our hands on. The best, of course, would be to use a manuscript. Short

Figure A.1 *Nacht und Träume*, Franz Schubert

of that, there's every good reason to trust Urtext editions. We are getting probably the greatest amount of truth from them, short of us getting to the manuscript. I don't have that here, though, but this is the old [Eusebius] Mandyczewski nineteenth-century edition.

I notice immediately that the piece is only two pages long. I've often said, "Be very careful with a composer who writes short songs." Look out for Schubert. He's a tricky man. That which he puts on one page is oftentimes the most difficult to lift off. Wagner holds us captive for days on end in the Ring Cycle—days on end to make his point. Schubert makes a point probably no less profound on one page.

As a side note, I always wish that performers would examine the score first and deal with that before listening to a recording. Because, ultimately, when I'm working with a student, I want an outcome that belongs to the student. I want the student's stamp on the performance. I know Elly Ameling's performance. I know Fischer-Dieskau's performance. I know Gerald Moore's performance of it at the piano. I know the thoughts of Martin Isepp from his playing of the piece. I don't need them again. I only want Martin Isepp when Martin Isepp steps up and plays this. But until then, I want you [the student] to put a stamp on this piece. What are your thoughts? I may agree with them;

I may not agree with them. It doesn't matter. But what is your take on this piece? And that's where it needs to come from. And it's really good that, historically speaking, as much information as we have about this piece, we don't have any more. Because I want, ultimately, your reading of this poem with these designated pitches and rhythms. Your ideas are valued.

So, how about we get moving from left to right in this music? The first thing I notice is the key signature. Schubert was very well known for writing multiple versions of his songs. But the original, in this case, is B major. It's important to know that, whether you're going to sing it in B major or not.

Students many times would ask me in song literature courses, "Do you think Schubert knew what he was doing?" You mean, you think Schubert was doing something mindlessly? Well, we have his record of 610 songs. So, yes, I think he knew what he was doing. He purposely set this in B major. We can maybe assume it was for a reason relating to the text, but we don't know for certain.

As teachers, we have to be very careful about speaking on behalf of a dead composer. If some historical information—a letter, perhaps—indicates that Schubert made some statements about this piece when writing it, we can then share that information with our students. Until then, all we have to deal with is the score.

I even want to check to make certain that the correct poet has been cited. Publishers can make mistakes, too. This lists Matthius von Collin as the poet. I have read that there are some who attribute the poem to Schiller. We have to try to find that out. Again, the Urtext may give us that information or will provide some historical notes. We have to be careful in checking, as I hope you will do with my work. Check it out and verify it.

The first thing I see in the music, before the key signature, actually, is that the clefs provided for the piano are both F [bass] clefs. Unbelievable! When I see that, my first thought is that very few German composers prior to Schubert were setting a piano accompaniment for a song with two F clefs. That strikes me and makes me wonder. In lifting this off the page, I have to find a purpose for that choice. Why would he have set this so low in the piano? When I look at the text—and I don't want to put words in Schubert's mouth—there is a sense of longing, and a plea to allow these dreams that occur at night to come back. They leave with the day. They're going down with the sun and I yearn to have them back. By the very fact that the poem is about night and darkness, we might make that assumption.

Be careful of coaches who definitively say, "Schubert wrote this with two F clefs to depict the night." Unless someone wrote down what the man has stated, we don't know that. All we have to go by is the music. All I know for sure is that it's written with two F clefs.

Then I see in the music a written-out tremolando, which is important to me because I find it pedagogical. How would Schubert play a tremolando on the piano? Well, it's right here before me. You will find editions where the editors don't write out all the tremolando. They write it in more of a modern notation of whole notes for the length of the measure. But I find it interesting that Schubert writes out the tremolando. The pianist and I should at least have an awareness that it's there. Maybe that can serve as, if you will, the heartbeat of the poet, according to Schubert.

I can then look at this *sehr langsam* tempo marking and see how that relates to this text. *SEHR langsam*. Not just *langsam*, but *sehr langsam*. Besides that, there's no metronome marking, which leaves the door open. We've got this incredible tremolando, that keeps the peace—the heartbeat, if you will—and the rhythm of the piece going, even at this slow tempo. We have sixteen sixteenth notes in the right hand in any given bar of that tremolando and no two of those sixteenth notes are equal to each other by virtue of their position in the bar. So they can't be played the same way. Don't bore me. We know that music moves from left to right, so by the time you get over here [the right-hand side of the measure], you are not the same person as you were here [the start of the measure]. This gets back to "No Parking." Martin Katz once said in a master class, "There are no two rhythms that are alike. One is longer than the other." That's my point. So as this poem courses through your mind, under the influence of Schubert, you are at a different place as a performer here than you were there. And a singer and a pianist can distinguish themselves by their abilities to do this. That's the imagination. That gives you the chance to put your stamp on it.

At the same time, we still have to have some regularity of rhythm and we have a responsibility to play what's on the page. We can't change these sixteen notes to whole notes, for instance. There are designated pitches and rhythms and we have a re-spon-si-bility to perform them. We may decide to transpose them, but we have to also be very careful that the transposition is not going to interfere with what you deem the text to say. If you think the text has some darkness to it, some sadness to it, some longing to it, a prayer that these dreams return, to play it on the upper third of the piano may distort that meaning. So, in transposition, the chosen key is important.

Also, just to put this argument to rest, we still have a lot of voice teachers out here who want to assign repertoire as "male songs" or "female songs." I've heard some teachers say, "No man should be singing that song," or "No woman should be singing that song." Well, I don't see that direction here in the music. Nowhere on the page does it state that. There isn't even a dedicatory statement of "for so-and-so."

I used to get myself into some fun by asking students, "Who should sing *Frauenliebe und Leben*?" They usually didn't even have to think about it. "Oh," they would say, "only a female would understand those thoughts." Well, who wrote it? This isn't written by Clara Schumann. I see a set of nine songs—if you count the ninth song as the big postlude at the end—written by two men. One was the poet and the other was the composer. Same thing with *Dichterliebe*. That's utter foolishness.

Another thing that catches my eye here in the score are the alterations to the key signature. A key signature is very important. So when a composer strays from that, I notice. And so I wonder about that G natural that I see [in the fourth measure]. Is that possibly indicative of something that will occur later in the piece? That's one question that many times I will ask. How can the pianist lift that off the page and bring that to the attention of the listener to the benefit of the song and its text? You don't even have to be able to read music to hear that. If I'm actively listening, as soon as that flatting occurs, it strikes my ears and I have to ask how that tonality might fit into the text. As we find out, something is going away. And we will have to wait until the next night, or until the next moon for it to return. And until then, I may just have to pine.

What dreams this individual is dealing with, we don't know. And we cannot and should not assign a dream, because unless we've talked to Schubert or Collin, we don't know. But there is loss, and that is a human condition with which we can empathize. If we knew something about the poet at the time he wrote this, from a letter or some kind of a record, [there may be experiences with] lost love, death, losing a friend, losing a lover, losing a parent. We don't know, and it's not for us to spend a lot of time with that. What we do know is that there are dreams that the poet does not want to let go. And what we do know is that those dreams can possibly resurface when looking to the night sky—to the moon. We know that.

We also see that it's just not *die Nacht*. It's *heilige Nacht*. So it's a holy or sacred night. And you will also see—I'm not going to call it tone painting; Schubert didn't talk about tone painting so I'm not going to talk about tone painting—a descending direction of the melody in the voice. I think there's something significant about that. Did Schubert know what he was doing? Hell yes! Do you think he was a moron? Still, I'm not going to call that tone painting. I think that was assigned to Schubert by some musicologist who was trying to identify what the composer was doing. Until I read somewhere that Schubert said, "It's tone painting," then I'll believe it.

So, besides *heilige Nacht*, I'm going to start looking for adjectives, descriptive words, active verbs: descending, sinking—which is different from "lowering," to me.

Then I notice the intervallic relationship of the sixth. It is from *sinkest nieder* [in measures six and seven], which goes down into the bottom of the voice, which might even require, if a soprano or mezzo-soprano is singing this, to add some chest voice to lift that off the page. What? Chest voice? Yes. To see these things and to hear them is very, very important.

I also see some double dots in the rhythm [in measures five, twenty-one, and twenty-three]. That reminds me of the style of the French Baroque. That makes me wonder, and I would ask students, "I wonder to what extent Schubert had some knowledge of the French Baroque?" I don't know. I'm not going to say, "Oh, yes, he knew his music history." I don't know that. But I do know he's got a double dot there, so maybe that historical knowledge enters in.

Now, in the opening line of the voice, you've got the entire measure, short of one eighth note, to sit on a D-sharp. So what are you going to do during all that time? File your nails? When I go back to the text I see the first syllable of *heilige* is assigned to that long note. I don't know how many different sounds there are in there, but there are certainly more than just one pure vowel. If you're going to deal with just one vowel, you're likely to get caught parking. So you've [h], [ɑ], and all of the variations that you are taught never to sing from [ɑ] to [i]. My teachers always said, "Oh, don't spend any time between the vowels. You have to sit on the [ɑ] and then at the last moment you go to the secondary vowel." Not in my world. Schubert doesn't say that in the score. There's no direction in here that tells me how I am going to sing *heilige*. But I see an awful lot of sounds in there that I can use to paint the word "sacred," "holy," "divine." So I'm going to elongate all of those sounds for three-and-one-half beats. I've got the tremolando and I'm going to use every one of those sounds to underscore that adjective. And isn't it interesting that he devotes more time to the adjective than he does to the noun?

Look at the profundity of *nieder*. Again, he's given more time to the adverb than to the verb. Before I get to the second syllable, I will not have parked on any one sound. He's thrown the whole deck of cards of sounds in my hand: the jack, the ace in the hole, and the wildcard, too. So I'm going to use all of those sounds. But before I can use them, I've got to be aware of them. And because my understanding of *heilige* is not yours, nor should my understanding of *heilige* become yours, no one will use those sounds the way I do or the way you do.

Part of what makes this song so difficult is that you are sitting there so vocally exposed—practically bare naked. Schubert piles the difficulties on. *Sehr langsam*! And it's also very difficult to listen to when someone parks, as if it's just a machine forming those sounds. I must work to bring interest to this music, to lift it off the page, to bring you into the poem and the pitches and rhythms—not to bring you into me, but into the song. I *must* do that. And I *want* to do that. So my mind must be clear enough, without any distractions, that I have the will and the comfort to give my full attention to this difficult music.

The great singer Barbara Cook once said, "Be as authentic as we know how to be at the moment, so that we can be more and more present in what we do. The more we can do that, the safer we are." When I saw that quote, I knew I wouldn't live long enough to ever be able to bring forth a thought with that much meaning. So, imagine this whole piece of music. By the time you get to the double bar at the end, I should be changed. That's the goal. And that has nothing to do with you. It has everything to do with this music—this record of music right here.

The problem is, it feels dangerous to do that. What I ask people to do is what Barbara Cook did so well, which is, in effect, to undress emotionally. That's very frightening and new. But this very thing that seems most dangerous, as she says, is where safety lies. I buy that.

But that's what it's about. It isn't about just technique. It isn't just about physiology and anatomy. It's not just analyzing a piece of music. But all of that put together gives us the tools to lift these thoughts off the page, which coursed through the mind of—I think we can say—a great thinker. By the time we're done, we will have awakened the dead—we've taken the listener to another place. That's a huge responsibility. And when I realized that, it was a huge epiphany. The thought of getting on stage for my own self went out the window. I didn't have time for myself. And it became easier, actually, to perform because then I didn't have to worry about myself. The job was greater than myself.

I would say that this piece would even provoke a nonmusician. My mother, for instance, knew nothing about music other than singing a hymn in church. She had no formal training. But, had she heard this piece, she could have said, "That piece kind of makes me nervous. It upsets me a bit." She didn't need to understand a thing about how the key isn't established at the beginning, or how it feels harmonically unresolved in places. But she would probably be moved to want to hear it again.

We have a good poem. We have a good organization of pitches and rhythms here, which provokes even nonmusicians to say the song changed them, enlightened them. That's why this is an art song.

Another significant thing—when you look through this piece you can make an argument that it doesn't even end with a perfect authentic cadence. Why is that? Is something left unresolved? In the rules of tonal music, you would fail in music theory if you close the piece out without a perfect authentic cadence. If you go over to the close of the B section, for a sixteenth-note value, we get a perfect authentic cadence at the end of *stille, stille Brust* [measures thirteen and fourteen]. We get a B major cadence. But it's only for one-quarter of the measure. To have a perfect authentic cadence, you've got to have the tonic in the top voice and the bottom voice and a five-seven [chord] before it, or at least a five chord. Technically, it is there. But theoretically, I'd say I'm not hearing it long enough for it to register as a perfect authentic cadence.

So how are we going to look at that as a performer? How are we going to lift that off the page? We're not resolving harmonically, so does the poetic thought ever resolve? It comes back. We have another chance with each new moon. When is it resolved? Well, it's always descending and then ascending again until the morning the sun burns out. According to solar scientists, the sun is good for about another five billion years. So I guess you should get up in the morning, have your coffee, and be thankful.

Then, of course, it's typical for Schubert to move to another key in the relationship of a third. Here, that happens to be the flat six [G major]. I don't ever recall Bach doing that. I don't remember Handel doing that. There may be an example somewhere, but I don't think that Bach or Handel went that far in harmony. The flat six? If that doesn't strike you, I don't know what will. And, by the way, he doesn't resolve that, either. He doesn't have a clear perfect authentic cadence. It's not that he's changing to G major. It relates back to B major through that relationship of a third—we still have a tonal relationship happening.

Textually, it's the most positively forward-looking part of the poem in this B section. We see the contour of the melodic movement rising, ascending for a period of time, with hope for tomorrow. It's kind of a sad thought, really. We see in so many of Schubert's song texts a looking forward. Happiness is in the future. We don't know if Schubert himself was unhappy, but we do often see him selecting texts where happiness is in the future.

Again, did Schubert know what he was doing when constructing all of this? I can tell you this as a scripter: ink and paper were not cheap. Ink had to be made by hand for his pen, and he had to pay for it. Vellum was not cheap. Schubert was not going to put notes on paper without some good, clear sense of what he was doing.

I'm going back again to "No parking." I don't know if there is such a phrase as "dictional speech," but we could coin one. Under my rules of diction, I can take advantage of a myriad of sounds in the word *belauschen*. All of the sounds of the middle syllable, [l-ɑ-u], are assigned to a quarter note. Since I don't have any orchestra to sing over and cover me up, I can use all of those sounds to draw my listener into the poem, into the song. Since Schubert gave me that text, I'm going to take advantage of what he handed to me. Why would I not use that [l] sound and all of the intermediary sounds, the bridging sounds between the [l] and the [ɑ], and the bridging sounds between the [ɑ] and the [u]? I was told as a singer not to do that. But I thought, "You know what? If Ms. Schwarzkopf is doing that, I get to do it."

And remember, in my book, there are no two rhythms here that are equal to each other. If you want to lift this off the page, with your stamp on this performance, you get to decide, for example, which of these two quarter notes of *belauschen* you wish to stress. One is going to be longer and one's going to be shorter. That's all part of the rules of text rhythm within music. There are no two rhythms that are alike. The quarter note on *-schen* is on the second beat in the measure. It's not at the head of the bar. So, by position alone, it's not the same quarter-note value as the one before it.

I buy into the ideas of the late great collaborative pianist Gerald Moore. In his book *Am I Too Loud?* he talks about the accent marks in Schubert. He actually believes they are not traditional accents but instead what he calls a "time stress." I like that. Meaning, where there's an accent, you don't come down with a hammer and beat the note on the head, like you might with a Verdi accent. In Schubert, if the accent marking is above the quarter note, you would stretch the value of that quarter note, maybe by adding a bit of a dot. With *belauschen*, you can stretch the second syllable, which is stressed, and then shorten the weak syllable. It still adds up to two beats in time.

Later in that phrase [in measure sixteen], Schubert gives two notes to *mit* and writes the second as a D-natural. Even though it's in a weak beat of the measure, I'm going to stress that a bit to bring out the new tonality. That D-natural is going to get a little extra time from me. If it was worth Schubert the cost of some walnut-juice ink to put that on paper and vellum, by God, I'm going to give it a little bit more ink, too. I always said to students, "Every drop of ink on a score, you want to lift off the page. Every drop of it."

And then we have the repetition of text, which is so often ignored by singers. Every time it was ignored in my voice studio, I just about went through the roof. I'd say, "Did you notice you just repeated a line of text? Are you so entranced by the Xerox machine? You just sang a complete carbon copy of the previous phrase!"

Here, Schubert repeats the text a fourth higher. That gives us a C-natural in addition to a G-natural and a D-natural. That's a lot of ink. So, in this repetition, you've got diction, you've got tone changes, and you've got scale degree changes that you can use. You can even take the liberty of adding a time stress to highlight certain syllables. What you select to do is based upon what you want to say to your listener at that moment of repetition.

When your wife asks you, "Brian, will you do the dishes?" She doesn't tell you when, she doesn't tell you how. She just asks, "Will you do the dishes?" Let's say that it was at nine o'clock in the morning. Four o'clock rolls around. "Brian, I asked you this morning to do the dishes." You still procrastinate. Now it's 8:30 at night and the dishes are still there. "For God's sake, do the dishes, you fool!" I'll bet each repetition of that phrase would receive a different expression. You wouldn't have to come to me to figure out her meaning.

I have to believe all of these details composers give us are absolutely intentional. And we have the tools as learned musicians, and the duty, to pause and give our attention to these details. It wasn't just, "Oh, I'm gonna put a D-natural in there because it feels good." If I spent nearly forty years of my life in music only to find out that someone such as Schubert composed music along those lines, I would have wasted my time. How cheap. Then it's no longer art music. That's just doing whatever will move the emotions so I can pad my pockets with a lot of money.

Until I find that out, I'm going to continue to look at things this way. As Professor Bjorksten brought to my attention in many different ways through her teaching, when something strikes my ears, I want to find out what the composer is doing. And, in order to do this, you have to train yourself to actively listen to music.

Now, that doesn't mean you cannot turn the hi-fi off when you're tired of listening. If you're listening to a Beethoven symphony, and you get to the end of the first movement, and something comes into your mind that prevents you from continuing to listen actively, then stop. You don't need to imprison yourself by this art. But you've got to be able to listen in a way that, when you hear these things, they upset you. That D-natural upsets you. Maybe in a good way, maybe in a bad way. But I should be drawn to that alteration. And if that doesn't cause you to pause, find another job. Don't waste your time in music.

All of these details have to be noticed before they can be practiced and used when lifting the music off the page. And to do it selflessly. The last thing we want to do is to allow our egos to get involved here. But you are allowed to have a bit of individualism, as long as it's following the pianist's and singer's joint goal to lift the music off the page, selflessly, without creating musical discord and confusion to the listener.

That's how I taught.

Note

1 Editor: Eusebius Mandyczewski (1875–1929); Publisher Info: Schubert's Werke, Serie XX, Band 8. 1823–27, No.470 (pp. 68–9), Leipzig: Breitkopf & Härtel, 1895. Plate F.S. 829; Reprinted: New York: E. F. Kalmus, No.1088, n.d. (1965).—#16396; Copyright: Public Domain. https://imslp.org/wiki/Nacht_und_Tr%C3%A4ume,_D.827_(Schubert,_Franz).

Appendix II
A Brief Timeline of the Life and Career of Dr. Robert J. Harrison

September 29, 1949—Born in Dodgeville, Wisconsin, to Donald Carkeek Harrison (1924–99) and Verda Jayne (Evans) Harrison (1923–2021)

1967—Graduated from Dodgeville High School, enrolled at Milton College, Milton, Wisconsin

1971—Graduated from Milton College with a Bachelor of Arts degree in Music Performance

1971—Moved to New York City, worked as a professional chorister

1972—Married Sandra Lee Rezin (two daughters: Joanna Grace Harrison Etshokin and Liliana Marie Harrison Shearon and her spouse, William M. Shearon; two grandchildren: Violet Madelaine Shearon and Liam Christopher Shearon)

1976—Moved to Madison, Wisconsin, to begin graduate studies

1978—Graduated from the University of Wisconsin-Madison with a Master of Music degree in Voice Performance

1978–79—Visiting Professor, University of Wisconsin-Oshkosh

1979–80—Visiting Professor, Wichita State University, Kansas

1980–81—Visiting Professor, University of Arkansas, Fayetteville

1981—Hired as Assistant Professor, University of Colorado Boulder

1984–86—On leave from the University of Colorado to return to graduate school at the University of Arizona, where he completed the Doctor of Musical Arts degree in Vocal Performance with a minor in Musicology

1995—Promoted to Associate Professor

2002—Served as master teacher for the NATS Intern Program, Boise State University

2003—Promoted to Full Professor

2004—Accepted a position as Professor of Voice at the Indiana University School of Music, later named the Jacobs School of Music in 2005

2015—Retired from Indiana University at age sixty-five

Appendix III
Final Quotes

"Music is a remarkable language. It may be the greatest language. The very idea that you can communicate to people through organized sound, designated pitches and rhythms, and stir somebody emotionally—that's profound."

"What I'm asking you to do, what I believe is important, is that everything that comes out of your mouth as a performer has a purpose. And this is where you get to be creative."

"You can get gestures later. If you don't put it in the voice first, add a character in the voice first, and tell us about that character with your voice, there's no gesture that'll help. They're useless. Through the voice. Always through the voice."

"We don't want to know about your day. I don't need to know about your problems. I'm coming in with enough as a listener. Feel what you feel. That's fine. But, when you're on stage, I'm interested in something else—the poem, the music, and what they say. Demonstrate your thinking through this. I will know how you feel when you sing. That's all I need to know. The responsibility is not to ourselves, but to the words and the music. Be truthful. Change me. Enrich me."

"You owe the audience honesty, you owe them sincerity. And that means that you are honest with the composer and the librettist, the poet—you owe that to them, to represent them. At the same time, be yourself and present the character with all kinds of honesty."

"Going back to the first time I heard Schwarzkopf, she threw me over the edge, her singing, what she was doing, the sound of her, the sight of her, the movements that I could see, how she was changing and altering sound and the control of sound, how she walked on the stage—all of that affected me very profoundly. There was nothing that evening that could distract my ears and my eyes. And the feeling that I had in listening to her and watching her— she did things to my mind and my heart that are indescribable. That's what kept me learning. That's what drove me to become an outstanding student, because I still have that reaction today when I listen to a piece of music. When I add the intellectual tier to that, I can get out of control. I don't understand why others don't."

"Now, hopefully you're getting something from this. If not, cut it off."

"Just because I'm giving the directions now doesn't mean that what I'm saying is better than what someone else says."

"Take note, that the final assessment is here [holds up a sheet of music]."

"And remember not to allow the bastards to grind you down!" (**Noli nothis permittere te terere!**)—as shared with Bob by CU Professor Howard B. Waltz

Bibliography

American Academy of Teachers of Singing. "In Support of Fact-Based Voice Pedagogy and Terminology." *Journal of Singing* 71, no. 1 (2014): 9–14.

Austin, Stephen F. *Provenance: Historic Voice Pedagogy Viewed through a Contemporary Lens.* Gahanna, OH: Inside View Press, 2017.

Bachner, Louis. *Dynamic Singing: A New Approach to Free Voice Production.* New York, NY: A. A. Wyn, Inc., 1944.

Ben-Sira, Zeev. "Affective and Instrumental Components in the Physician-patient Relationship: An Additional Dimension of Interaction Theory." *Journal of Health and Social Behavior* 21 (1980): 170–80.

Ben-Sira, Zeev. "The Function of the Professional's Affective Behavior in Client Satisfaction: A Revised Approach to Social Interaction Theory." *Journal of Health and Social Behavior* 17 (1976): 3–11.

Benson, Elizabeth Ann. *Training Contemporary Commercial Singers.* Braunton, UK: Compton Publishing Ltd., 2020.

Benson, Elizabeth Ann, and Kate Rosen. "Anti-Fat Bias in the Singing Voice Studio, Part Two: How to Make a Size Inclusive Voice Studio." *Journal of Singing* 79, no. 5 (2023): 653–60. https://doi.org/10.53830/KNDP8249.

Berry, Wendell. "The Momentum of Clarity." In *The Geography of Hope: A Tribute to Wallace Stegner*, edited by Page Stegner and Mary Stegner. San Francisco, CA: Sierra Club Books, 1996.

Bigler, Amelia Rollings, Katherine Osborne, Chadley Ballantyne, Brian Horne, Kimberly James, Brian Manternach, Yvonne Redman, and Melissa Treinkman. "Voice Pedagogy for the 21st Century: The Summation of Two Summits." *Journal of Singing* 78, no. 1 (2021): 11–28. https://dx.doi.org/10.53830/cxbg6722.

Bozeman, Kenneth W. *Practical Vocal Acoustics:Pedagogic Applications for Teachers and Singers.* Lanham, MD: Rowman & Littlefield Publishing, 2022.

Chapman, Gary. *The Five Love Languages: How to Express Heartfelt Commitment to Your Mate.* Chicago, IL: Northfield Publishing, 1992.

Clemmons, Jo. "Rapport and Motivation in the Applied Studio." *Journal of Singing* 63, no. 2 (2006): 205–10.

Coates, Shannon. "Neurodiversity in the Voice Studio, Clinic, and Performance Space: Using a Neurodiversity Affirming Lens to Build More Inclusive Spaces for Singers, Part 1, Current Understanding of Neurodiversity." *Journal of Singing* 79, no. 2 (2022): 213–19. https://doi.org/10.53830/VHSX6387.

Cowgill, Jennifer Griffith. "Breathing for Singers: A Comparative Analysis of Body Types and Breathing Tendencies." *Journal of Singing* 66, no. 2 (2009): 141–7.

Davis, Viola. "Viola Davis: All Artists have 'Imposter Syndrome.'" *60 Minutes*, December 6, 2020. YouTube, 3:07. https://www.youtube.com/watch?v=xc3bKzrz4D4.

Doscher, Barbara M. *The Functional Unity of the Singing Voice, 2nd Edition Expanded with an Introduction by John Nix.* Lanham, MD: Rowman & Littlefield Publishing, 2023.

Draina, Barbara. *The Breathing Book for Singers.* Flagstaff, AZ: Mountain Peak Music, 2019.

Edwards, Matthew. "Mix it up Monday: Thinking About Body Type and Age when Teaching Breath Management." *EdwardsVoice*, November 6, 2017. https://edwardsvoice.wordpress.com/2017/11/06/mix-it-up-monday-thinking-about-body-type-and-age-when-teaching-breath-management/.

Francis, Vida, Barbara M. Korsch, and Marie J. Morris. "Gaps in Doctor-patient Communication: Patients' Response to Medical Advice." *New England Journal of Medicine* 280, no. 10 (1969): 535–40.

Helding, Lynn. *The Musician's Mind: Teaching, Learning, and Performance in the Age of Brain Science.* Lanham, MD: Rowman & Littlefield Publishing, 2020.

Helding, Lynn. "Science-Informed Vocal Pedagogy: Motor Learning, Deliberate Practice and the Challenge of Cognitive Dissonance." In *The Routledge Companion to Interdisciplinary Studies in Singing, Volume II: Education*, edited by Helga R. Gudmundsdottir, Carol Beynon, Karen Ludke, and Annabel J. Cohen. Routledge Publishing, 2020.

Hoit, Jeannette D., and Thomas J. Hixon. "BodyType and Speech Breathing." *Journal of Speech and Hearing Research* 29, no. 3 (1986): 313–24.

Iwarsson, Jenny, and Johan Sundberg. "Effects of Lung Volume on Vertical Larynx Position during Phonation." *Journal of Voice* 12, no. 2 (1998): 159–65.

Korsch, Barbara M., Ethel K. Gozzi, and Vida Francis. "Gaps in Doctor-patient Communication: I. Doctor-patient Interaction and Patient Satisfaction." *Pediatrics* 42, no. 5 (1968): 855–71.

Korsch, Barbara M., and Vida Francis Negrete. "Doctor-patient Communication." *Scientific American* 227, no. 2 (1972): 66–75.

Mandyczewski, Eusebius, ed. *Schubert's Werke, Serie XX, Band 8. 1823-27, No.470 (pp. 68-69)*. Leipzig: Breitkopf & Härtel, 1895. Plate F.S. 829; Reprinted: New York: E. F. Kalmus, No.1088, n.d.(1965). - #16396; Copyright: Public Domain. https://imslp.org/wiki/Nacht_und_Tr%C3%A4ume,_D.827_(Schubert,_Franz).

Manternach, Brian. "George Gagnidze: Baritone Back in Business." *Classical Singer*, January/February 2022, 24–5.

Manternach, Brian. "Master of None: Challenging the Master-Apprentice Model." *Journal of Singing* 80, no. 4 (2024): 447–54. https://doi.org/10.53830/sing.00028.

Manternach, Brian. "Neil Shicoff: A Force for 40 Years." *Classical Singer,* September 2018, 46–7.

Manternach, Brian, and David Eggers. "Using Theatrical Intimacy Practices to Create Vocal Health Boundaries." *Journal of Singing* 79, no. 1 (2022): 73–7. https://doi.org/10.53830/TUBl6925.

Manternach, Jeremy N. "Effects of Varied Conductor Prep Movements on Singer Muscle Engagement and Voicing Behaviors." *Psychology of Music* 44, no. 3 (2016): 574–86. doi:10.1177/0305735615580357.

Manternach, Jeremy N. "The Effect of Varied Conductor Preparatory Gestures on Singer Upper Body Movement." *Journal of Music Teacher Education* 22, no. 1 (2012): 20–34. doi:10.1177/1057083711414428.

Meyer, David, and Lynn Helding. "Practical Science in the Studio: 'No-Tech' Strategies." *Journal of Singing* 77, no. 3 (2021): 360.

Miller, Richard. "The Singing Teacher in the Age of Voice Science." In *Vocal Health and Pedagogy*, 3rd ed., edited by Robert Sataloff. Plural Publishing, Inc., 1991.

Monti, Elisa, Megan Durham, and Allison Reynolds. "Focusing the Scope: The Voice Practitioner's Role in Trauma-Informed Care." *Journal of Singing* 80, no. 4 (2024): 455–62. https://doi.org/10.53830/sing.00029.

National Association of Teachers of Singing. "NATS Science-Informed Voice Pedagogy Institute." https://www.nats.org/Science-Informed_Pedagogy_Institute.html (accessed November 20, 2024).

National Association of Teachers of Singing. "Science-Informed Voice Pedagogy Resources." https://www.nats.org/cgi/page.cgi/Science-Informed_Voice_Pedagogy_Resources.html (accessed November 20, 2024).

Nix, John. "Best Practices: Using Exercise Physiology and Motor Learning Principles in the Teaching Studio and the Practice Room." *Journal of Singing* 74, no. 2 (2017): 215–20.

Perna, Nicholas, and Sarah Pigott. "The Breathing Episode." *VocalFri Podcast*, September 26, 2019, 29:18–34:49. https://www.vocalfri.com/e/the-breathing-episode/.

Ragan, Kari. *A Systematic Approach to Voice: The Art of Studio Application*. San Diego, CA: Plural Publishing, 2020.

Ragan, Kari. "Defining Evidence-Based Voice Pedagogy: A New Framework." *Journal of Singing* 75, no. 2 (2018): 157–60.

Rojahn, Susan Young. "Memory Is Inherently Fallible, and That's a Good Thing." *MIT Technology Review*, October 9, 2013. https://www.technologyreview.com/2013/10/09/176152/memory-is-inherently-fallible-and-thats-a-good-thing/.

Rosenberg, Marci, and Wendy D. LeBorgne. *The Vocal Athlete: Application and Technique for the Hybrid Singer*, 3rd ed. San Diego, CA: Plural Publishing, 2024.

Scearce, Leda. *Manual of Singing Voice Rehabilitation: A Practical Approach to Vocal Health and Wellness*. San Diego, CA: Plural Publishing, 2016.

Sherwood, Travis. "Evolving the Master-Apprentice Tradition: A Pathway Back to a Student-Centered Pedagogy." *Journal of Singing* 80, no. 1 (2023): 13–22. https://doi.org/10.53830/GTOJ3285.

Small, Christopher. *Musicking: The Meanings of Performing and Listening*. Middletown, CT: Wesleyan University Press, 1998.

Sundberg, Johan. "Breathing Behavior During Singing." *The NATS Journal* 49, no. 3 (1993): 4–9, 49–51.

The Voice Lab. "Gender-Affirming Speech and Singing at The Voice Lab." https://thevoicelabinc.thinkific.com/courses/gender-affirming-voice-and-speech-spring-2024 (accessed November 20, 2024).

Titze, Ingo R. "On Flow Phonation and Airflow Management." *Journal of Singing* 72, no. 1 (2015): 57–8.

Titze, Ingo R. *Principles of Voice Production*. Iowa City, IA: National Center for Voice and Speech, 2000.

Titze, Ingo R. "The Five Best Vocal Warm-up Exercises." *Journal of Singing* 57, no. 3 (2001): 51–2.

Titze, Ingo R. "The Language and Basic Phenomena of Nonlinear Dynamics in Vocal Fold Vibration." *Journal of Singing* 76, no. 3 (2020): 295–7.

Titze, Ingo R. "Voice Training and Therapy with a Semioccluded Vocal Tract: Rationale and Scientific Underpinnings." *Journal of Speech, Language, and Hearing Research* 49, no. 2 (2006): 448–59. https://doi.org/10.1044/1092-4388(2006/035).

Titze, Ingo R., and Katherine Verdolini Abbott. *Vocology: The Science and Practice of Voice Habilitation*. Salt Lake City, UT: National Center for Voice and Speech, 2010.

Titze Cox, Karin, and Ingo R. Titze. *Voice is Free After SOVT*. Clearfield, UT: National Center for Voice and Speech, 2023.

Westerman, Kenneth N. *Emergent Voice*. Ann Arbor, MI: Self-published, 1947.

Contributors

Brian Manternach (he/him) is an associate professor (clinical) at the University of Utah Department of Theatre and a research associate for the Utah Center for Vocology, where he is on the faculty of the Summer Vocology Institute. He earned a B.A. in music from Saint John's University/College of Saint Benedict in Minnesota, a Master of Music in vocal performance from the University of Wisconsin-Milwaukee, and a Doctor of Music degree in Voice Performance and Literature from the Indiana University Jacobs School of Music.

Honors include the Teacher of the Year Award from the Cal-Western Region of the National Association of Teachers of Singing (NATS), the NATS Foundation Voice Pedagogy Award, the NATS Clifton Ware Group-Voice Pedagogy Award, the Faculty Excellence in Research Award from the University of Utah College of Fine Arts, and the University of Utah Distinguished Teaching Award. He has presented research, lectures, and workshops for the Pan American Vocology Association, Voice Foundation Annual Symposium, International Physiology and Acoustics of Singing Conference, Voice and Speech Trainers Association, Fall Voice Conference, International Congress of Voice Teachers, Interdisciplinary Society for Quantitative Research in Music and Medicine, Voice Study Centre, TEDxSaltLakeCity, and for NATS at chapter, district, regional, and national conferences.

As an author, he is an associate editor of the *Journal of Singing*, writing and editing "The Independent Teacher" column. He is also a regular columnist for *Classical Singer* magazine, which has published more than 130 of his essays, interviews, and reviews. His additional articles have been published in the *Journal of Voice*, *Voice and Speech Review*, *VOICEPrints*, *NATS Inter Nos*, *College Music Symposium*, *Music Theatre Educators' Alliance Journal*, and the *Salt Lake Tribune*. He is a contributing author to four books, and he coauthored a paper that received the "Forum Article of the Year Award" from the *Voice and Speech Review*.

As a performer, Dr. Manternach's staged roles range from Belmonte in *Die Entführung aus dem Serail* to Eisenstein in *Die Fledermaus* to Miles Gloriosus in *A Funny Thing Happened on the Way to the Forum*. He has made solo appearances with the Milwaukee Symphony Orchestra, Cleveland Chamber Symphony, and Sinfonia Salt Lake, among others. He is a frequent music director and orchestra conductor for stage productions throughout the Salt Lake Valley. brianmanternach.com

Erika Edberg Manternach (she/her) has had a varied career in journalism, music, education, and writing. She spent ten years as anchor/reporter for TV stations in Rapid City, South Dakota; South Bend, Indiana; and Salt Lake City, Utah. After stepping away from broadcast journalism, she spent six years as a middle school and high school teacher, teaching courses in English, journalism, theology, and music. She was one of three finalists for the 2013 Journalism Educator of the Year Award by Youth Journalism International and earned the 2014 Employee of the Year Award for Juan Diego Catholic High School.

As a musician, she has served for more than thirty years as organist, pianist, choral director, and music director for churches, schools, and colleges.

Since 2015, she has worked for the AncestryProGenealogists® division of *Ancestry.com*, currently serving as the Publications Team Manager and previously as Senior Writer and Writing Team Manager. She conducts oral history interviews, writes family history books and narratives, and manages a team of writers, copyeditors, and graphic designers.

Born and raised in Minnesota, she holds B.A. degrees in Communication (Media Studies) and Music (Liturgical Music/Organ) from the College of Saint Benedict/Saint John's University. She holds a Certificate in Copyediting from the University of California San Diego.

She works as a freelance copyeditor, volunteers as a cat and kitten foster for Best Friends Animal Society of Utah, and rather dislikes used toothpicks being left around the house.

Tenor **Brian Horne** is the chair of the Department of Voice at the Indiana University Jacobs School of Music, where he specializes in studio voice and voice pedagogy.

He holds a bachelor's degree from Hiram College in Ohio, and master's and doctoral degrees from the Jacobs School. He previously taught at the University of Missouri and Shorter College and continues to perform and present master classes.

Horne's former students perform at venues such as the Metropolitan Opera, Houston Grand Opera, Canadian Opera Company, Santa Fe Opera, Opera Memphis, Atlanta Opera, Lyric Opera of Chicago, and Bayerische Staatsoper (Munich), as well as with symphonies such as those of Colorado, Indianapolis, Cincinnati, Melbourne, and Cleveland. In addition, they have sung leading roles on Broadway in shows such as *Rock of Ages*, *Groundhog Day*, and *Spiderman: Turn Out the Dark*.

Horne's students have won competitions such as the Cardiff Singer of the World, Metropolitan Opera National Council Auditions, $10,000 first prize in the National Association of Teachers of Singing (NATS) Artist Awards, and awards including Outstanding Performer in the Kennedy Center American College Theater Festival and the Shreveport Opera Singer of the Year.

His students have been finalists in the Houston Grand Opera Eleanor McCollum competition, Music Teachers National Association Young Artist competition, Dallas Opera Guild competition, Opera Columbus Irma Cooper Vocal Competition, and Mobile Opera Competition. They have also won career grants from the Richard Tucker and Merola foundations.

Students of Horne have participated in summer programs such as Tanglewood, Wolf Trap, Merola, Central City Opera, Opera Theatre of St. Louis, Opera New Jersey, and Des Moines Metro Opera, as well as in professional training programs such as the Academy of Vocal Arts and the Houston Opera Studio.

As faculty sponsor of the Student NATS chapter at Indiana University, professor of doctoral voice pedagogy courses, and research director for doctoral dissertations, Horne has mentored dozens of students into college teaching positions.

He was chosen to serve as a master teacher for the 2014 NATS Intern Program and is a member of the prestigious American Academy of Teachers of Singing.

Index

Note: Page numbers followed by 'n' indicate note numbers; page numbers in *italics* refers to figures.

acoustics   105–6, 134
agility   106–7, 112
alignment, *see* posture
Ameling, Elly   40, 75, 162
Anthony, James   39
Appleman, Ralph   147
Arroyo, Martina   34
art song
   definition of   61–66, 168
articulation
   consonants   80–1, 97, 99, 141
   vowels   80–1, 101, 103–8, 113, 166
artist
   definition of   64–5
artistry
   developing and teaching   73–5, 79–82
Arvin, Gary   41
Austin, Stephen F.   162, 174

Baker, Janet   24, 79
Benson, Elizabeth Ann   86–7
Bernstein, Leonard   34, 61
Berry, Walter   22
Berry, Wendell   157–8
Bjorksten, Bettina   *34*, 35–6, 38, 68, 120, 149–50, 158, 171
breathing, *see* respiration
Brubeck, Dave   34

Callas, Maria   74, 79, 127
characteristics of a good student   131–3
characteristics of a good teacher   133–135

Chiaroscuro   106, 108
choosing vocal exercises   112–14
citing sources   140–3
Clemmons, Jo   155
Coffin, Berton   2, 38, 91, 101, 103–5, 119, 142, 146
consonants, *see* articulation
Cook, Barbara   167
Cowgill, Jennifer Griffith
   "Breathing for Singers: A Comparative Analysis of Body Types and Breathing Tendencies"   87–88
Crumb, Dorothy   38
curiosity   20, 28, 52, 68, 116, 132–3
cynicism   74–78

Davis, Viola   122
detail
   attention to   54–57, 116, 171
   drawn in by   53–4
Dewese, Scott   11
Doscher, Barbara   2, 80, 99, 103–4, 107–8, 114–15, 146
Douglas, Nancy   57

eccentricities   49–51
Edwards, Matthew   88
Emmons, Shirlee   91–2, 103, 108, 142
emulation   6, 20, 149–51
Enya   63–5
   "How can I keep from singing?"   64
   "Sail away"   63–4
evaluating music   63–6
evaluating past teachers   145–8

failure 4, 36–7, 121, 140
Farrell, Eileen 147
Finley, Carolyn 11
Fioratura 107
Fischer-Dieskau, Dietrich 22–3, 75, 162
Fleming, Renée 24

Gagnidze, George 85
Gedda, Nicolai 22–3
generational trends in singing 75–8
Gilbert, Dale 119
Golden Rule 156
Gonzales Redman, Yvonne 37

Harrison, Donald Carkeek 17–18, 26–7, 54, 74, 131
Harrison, Sandy 22, 27, 35, 39–42, 51–3, 58
Harrison, Verda Jayne 17, 27, 131, 168
Helding, Lynn 25, 116, 133, 134
honesty 71, 141, 150, 174
Horne, Brian 13–14
Hotter, Hans 79
Howell, Ian 36–7

imposter syndrome 120–122
Indiana University Jacobs School of Music (IU) 2–3, 13–14, 26, 34, 40–3, *44*, 49, 70, 78, 112, 126, 147, 157, 173
influence 4–5, 26–8, 35, 65, 68, 70, 77–9, 141, 146, 149, 154–8
intellectual enlightenment 61–5, 168
Isepp, Martin 79–80, 82–3, 162

Jackson, Dennis 38

Katz, Martin 164
Kiesgen, Paul 40–1
Klemperer, Otto 22
known to the unknown 52, 90, 106, 111

Lamperti, Giovanni Battista 85
Lavonis, William 13
Legacy 153–4
listening
    importance of active listening 3, 22–3, 69, 106, 165, 171

musical listening parties 22–4, 116
    in teaching 111–12, 114–16
Ludwig, Christa 22–3

Manternach, Carolyn 29, *30*, 54–5, 57, 129, 156–7
Manternach, Erika Edberg xiv, 2, 42–3, *44*, 45, 55
Manternach, Jeremy 29, 95 n.17
Manternach, Jerry 20, 27, *28*, 29, *30*, 44–5, 55, 57, 129, 156–7
Messa di voce 107
Miller, Richard 134, 146
Milnes, Sherrill 119
Milton College 19, 22, 33, 116
Moore, Gerald 79–80, 82–3, 162
music as language 70, 90, 174
musical bias 65–8

Nacht und Träume
    analysis of 161–71
National Association of Teachers of Singing (NATS) 97, 112, 146, 155, 173
Newman, Arthur 38
Nix, John 113
No air, no sound, *see* respiration
No parking, *see* respiration
Norman, Jessye 81

Parsons, Geoffrey 23
Passaggio 97, 99–100, 112
Pears, Peter 22
performance as service 69–71
performing *vs.* teaching 14–15, 125–9
Perna, Nicholas 94 n.13
Peterson, Patti 12
phonation 87, 90, 94 n.13, 97–9
    balanced phonation 97, 99
    breath pressure *vs.* breath flow 86–8, 97–8, 103–9
    breathy phonation 94 n.13
    flow phonation 94 n.13, 98
    phonation threshold pressure 99
    pressed phonation 86, 94 n.13, 98
pop song
    definition of 63
posture 23, 89, 92

Poulimenos, Andreas   40
Pyle, Thomas   33

Queler, Eve   34

Ramey, Samuel   38
rapport   155
rejection   5, 36–7
resonance   94 n.13, 103–8, 115, 147
   forced resonance   59
   the "resonance valve"   103, 106–7
   "That really resonates with me"   59
respiration   84–91
   and body type   87–8
   breath pressure versus breath flow   86–8, 97–8, 103–9
   breathing vowels   104
   catch breath   89, 92–3
   in CCM genres   86–7
   as communication   90–1, 142
   conductor's breath   89
   no air, no sound   83, 85, 88, 93, 141
   no parking   83–4, 141, 164, 169
   "taking" a breath   89, 91–2
   tracheal pull   86–7
Richards, Gwyn   41–42

Sanborn, Thomas F.   22, 24, 33
Scearce, Leda   86
Schiller, Daniela   6
Schwarzkopf, Elizabeth   22–6, 74–5, 79–80, 89, 169, 174
semi-occluded vocal tract exercises (SOVTEs)   97–99, 113, 141
senses   53, 57–8, 61
Shaw, Robert   33–4

Shicoff, Neil   121
Shirley-Quirk, John   79
Small, Christopher   65
Smith, Gregg   34
Spillman, Robert   117
Starker, János   70, 127
Stegner, Wallace   157–158
Stokowski, Leopold   34
Strauss, Richard   24, 62
Streisand, Barbara   74, 79
Sundberg, Johan   86, 98

Titze, Ingo   86, 98–9, 106, 113, 155
Trunkhill, Marlys   33
truth, sharing the truth   51, 70–1, 120, 125–6, 140

University of Arizona   27, 38
University of Colorado Boulder (CU)   2, 11, 36, 38, 42, 61, 71, 80, 91, 104, 107, 114, 117, 146, 154, 172–3, 175

Vaness, Carol   126–127
Vennard, William   104, 119, 146
Verdolini Abbott, Katherine (Kittie)   122, 155
voice science   105, 146–8
von Stade, Frederica   40, 79
vowels, *see* articulation

Westerman, Kenneth   97, 103–4
Westerman Gregg, Jean   97
Westland, Bernie   52
White, Andrew B.   119
Wiederanders, William   33